Beginning to Grow

Beginning to Grow
Five Studies

Sylvia Brody, Ph.D

IPBOOKS
International Psychoanalytic Books

A Division of International Psychoanalytic Media Group

Beginning to Grow: Five Studies
All Rights Reserved.
Copyright © 2009 Sylvia Brody
v2.0

International Psychoanalytic Books
Arnold D. Richards, Editor
arniedr15@gmail.com

ISBN: 978-0-615-30581-3

Library of Congress Control Number: 2009927883

International Psychoanalytic Books and the International Psychoanalytic Books logo are trademarks belonging to Arnold D. Richards, Editor.

PRINTED IN THE UNITED STATES OF AMERICA

Table of Contents

Preface

One day when I was about ten, idly turning the pages of a women's magazine, I came upon an article entitled "Children Are People." I was astonished that someone else in the big world outside also realized this! By the time I was twelve, I was sure that if I were ever in a position to do anything about it, I would establish a law that no one could have a child without a license. I supposed it would take a long time to establish the requirements for obtaining one. Nevertheless, I was determined to find out how children could be saved from the confusions and impediments that I was continuously observing among them. So during the years of the Great Depression, in the 1930s, I began to make weekly excursions to the main branch of the New York Public Library, to read what I could about infant and child rearing. To my delight, I quickly found the shelf that included Bertrand Russell's *Education and the Good Life* (1926), Ethel Mannin's *Common Sense and the Child* (1931), A.S. Neill's *The Problem Child* (1932), and Fritz Wittel's *Set the Children Free* (1933). These books opened up a new world of information and thinking for me.

Then I discovered five schools in New York City at which the principles of education followed those of the authors I had read. As the rate of unemployment was great at the time, I chose to work as an unpaid assistant at the Walden School; probably I liked the literary allusion in its name. The director of that school, Elizabeth

Goldsmith, had been analyzed by Sandor Ferenczi, and upheld the principles of freedom for children, which contrasted sharply with the more formal educational rules that were then common, and in which I had been schooled. Soon, I was gladly surprised to be attending monthly lectures by psychoanalysts of the caliber of Bertram Lewin, Lawrence Kubie, Berta Bornstein, and Annie Reich, the latter two were among the newly arrived refugees from Nazi-occupied Eastern Europe. Along with other unpaid assistants, I also attended weekly lectures about infantile sexuality and unconscious conflict by a Hungarian psychoanalyst, Toscan Bennett. That was how I stumbled upon psychoanalysis.

A few years later, I left New York and went to work with troubled children at the Southard School of the Menninger Foundation in Kansas. I was invited to participate in the Infancy Research Project being carried out by Sybille Escalona, Ph.D. and Mary Leitch, M.D., where infants between the ages of four and twenty-eight weeks were observed in the presence of their mothers for individual differences at regular intervals. My observations of the experiential events that influence infant development brought me to concentrate on the maternal influences on development. I soon realized that the quality of an infant's experience can be known only in conjunction with knowledge about the quality of daily care afforded by the mother. Some on the Menninger staff warned that I could learn nothing about mothers from observing them with their infants; my observations soon contradicted that. My interest in the development of infants has continued to influence my clinical and research activities up to the present. I have seen again and again how experiences in the infants' and children's relationships with their parents influence early development. Paternal behavior is an area of research that has, until recently, barely been touched on.[1]

A world of psychoanalytic understanding of fathers and their influences on the infant and child still awaits study. My theoretical point of view has always lain in classical psychoanalysis. Beginning in 1956 with my first book, *Patterns of Mothering*, my study of the

---

[1] I have discussed this subject in two essays: 'The Father's Dilemma,' privately published in 1979 in Kassel, Germany, and 'Fathers in Nineteenth Century Novels: Some Portrayals of Unconscious Conflict in Paternal Attitudes and Behavior,' published by Little Brown in Father and Child: Development and Clinical Perspectives, eds. Cath, Gurwitt, and Ross, in 1982.

component instincts has grown out of continuous observations of parental behavior in infant and child development. In the following years, I have described the subjects of my further studies (which lasted from 1963 to 1983) from their births to age 7 (Brody & Axelrad 1970, 1978) and again at age 18 (Brody & Siegel 1992). Many of the subjects were described at age 30 by Henry Massie, M.D. and Nathan Szajnberg, M.D. (Massie & Szajnberg 2005). Psychological tests of the subjects at age 18 were carried out by Jan Drucker, Ph.D., Fran Luckom-Nurnberg, Ph.D., and Marsha Winokur, Ph.D. Fine interpretations of the subjects' drawings at ages 4, 5, and 18 were written by Sara Markese, Ph.D., prior to her having any knowledge of the subjects' histories. Once she had read the histories of the children, she made few emendations of her analyses.

During the writing of this book, I have at intervals received excellent secretarial help from Stacy Freyer Fevinger, Molly L. Quammen, Gabi Sifre, and J. Brooks Robinson, New York University graduates of the Gallatin School of Individualized Study, as well as Angelica A. Silva, also a NYU graduate of the College of Arts and Sciences. This book's cover image was designed by Brooks Robinson and me, and is comprised of drawings, at ages 5 and 18 (five year-olds' drawings in color, eighteen year-olds' in black and white), by subjects of my studies of infants, children, and their parents. I am grateful to Warren Poland, M.D., Professor Charles Hanly, and Arnold Richards, M.D., for their guidance at various periods throughout this writing. I am especially indebted to Dr. Richards for his general readiness to respond to questions about my work, whenever they arose. Unique personal support in my efforts throughout the writing of this book has come in dark times from my niece, Beth Puffer, and my dear friends Ludmila McKannay and Galina Alipova, who cheered me on.

—Sylvia Brody
September 26, 2008

INTRODUCTION

Introduction

When the scientific study of the child began in the decades between 1890 and 1910, there was still no course in any European college on the psychology of the child, but a growing circle of educators in Germany, France, England and the United States had turned their attention to the experimental study of child development and child mentality. In America, assorted papers on these subjects appeared from 1891 on, in the *Pedagogical Seminary*, a journal edited by G. Stanley Hall. In 1895, Dewey set up an experimental school in Chicago; in 1905 Freud published the *Three Contributions to the Theory of Sex*, which was followed in the next few years by his essays on the sexual theories of children. In 1908, Hall published his two volume work *Adolescence*. In 1909, Freud made the first attempt to analyze a child's neurosis. In the same year, Hall invited Freud to lecture at Clark University in Worcester. Freud was ever indebted to Hall for the impetus the American educator and psychologist gave to the acceptance of psychoanalysis here, and to the study of the child in many parts of the world. Freud referred to Hall's work on adolescence as signal in the history of our understanding of the sexuality of the child.

Educational methods at the turn of the century were based largely on sentiment and opinion. In child training, moral terms on one hand, and faculty development on the other, were still the vital considerations. This disturbed Claparède (1913), a French professor at the Geneva University. He asserted with some heat that teachers needed first of all to learn how to observe, and how to doubt their own set ideas about children. He called for a genetic psychology, and devalued the categorization of human faculties according to age. The question for him was how and why these faculties functioned. The largest part of his book[2] recalls his predecessors in the field and to what extent he must have been stimulated by them. For example, he took up the subject of "fatigue" in an effort to grasp the relationship between physical states and work capacity; Rousseau-like, he defended the child who was too sleepy to get up in the morning. That child was really accusing his teachers of their failure to interest him. Claparède gave form to the inchoate ideals of Pestalozzi (1894). Both were concerned with the harmonious development of "the whole child." In Volume X (1903) of the Pedagogical Seminary, the complexity of voluntary attention and its relation to fatigue was taken up. In all of these studies, the tone was remarkably sympathetic to the child; it was as if the adult world had suddenly become aware of a long-standing neglect of children's experiences and needs, and was now deeply eager to set matters right.

Hall had, as a college student, read Darwin and it was Darwin whom he gratefully acknowledged as an important source of his appreciation of genetic psychology. His continued study of evolutionary biology supported and energized his work on education. It was not until he realized that knowledge of biology and physiology could be integrated that his psychological ideas took form. Once he realized that in addition to the process of physical evolution there was a process of mental evolution he was able to envision a way to systematize a "genetic psychology." His journals from 1803-1903 indicated that the time was ripe for the psychoanalytic doctrines that followed so soon after.

William James, as the founder of the "Functional School" had

[2]*Experimental Pedagogy and the Psychology of the Child*

in 1890 concerned himself with the question of how emotional thought, sense perception and mental images fulfilled the needs of the human organism. As the century drew to a close, interest in the nature of infancy and childhood was high, and after Helen Keller (1903) published the story of her life, serious students in the fields of psychology and education were impressed by the broad possibilities for growth latent in every child. No longer was it sufficient to list stages of development mechanically; it was necessary to observe why children had particular interests, and why they had them with more or less intensity. Hall's concern for the development of a genetic approach led him to accept the concept of the unconscious, which he pioneered with and for Freud in America. His study reached a high mark when he came to New York to learn from Freud about instinctual development. The contributions made by him and his colleagues to the psychology of the child formed a bridge between the idealistic approach of the nineteenth century, and the empiricism of psychoanalysis in the twentieth. Until the past half-century psychological vulnerability during infancy was generally discounted. Underestimation of the impact of early experience was coupled with an overestimation of an infant's capacity to escape the effects of (seemingly) benign neglect. I have described notable exceptions to this history before (Brody, 1956; Brody & Axelrad, 1970; Brody & Siegel, 1992). The psychoanalytic study of infants was long regarded as lying outside the domain of psychoanalysis proper, because infants do not yet have sufficient language at their disposal. Among the assumptions about early development that have been brought forward in recent decades, some lack information about how and when the effects of early experience become manifest, some miss considerations of pathogenesis, some are imaginative but not demonstrable, and some are still being developed (Mayes, 1994).

I shall discuss briefly several subjects that in recent decades have influenced our understanding of relations between infantile experience and later psychological growth: theories of omnipotence in the infant, connections between early experience and later psychopathology, and the developmental approach. Following this discussion, I shall present the contribution to child development made by the component instincts (Freud 1905).

PAST CONCEPTS ABOUT EARLY CHILD DEVELOPMENT

1

Past Concepts about Early Child Development

Infant Feelings of Omnipotence

The idea of a subliminal wish for omnipotence was introduced by Freud (1909) when he described the phenomenon of omnipotence of thought in obsessional neurosis; in *Totem and Taboo* (1912) with regard to the seeming magical power of words; and in *Civilization and its Discontents* (1930), when he wrote "we cannot fail to recognize that the satisfaction of the instinct is accompanied by an extraordinarily high degree of narcissistic enjoyment, owing to its presenting the ego with a fulfillment of the latter's old wishes for omnipotence" (p.121). Ferenczi (1913) drew upon Freud's concept of omnipotence of thought to suggest that there is an ideal stage in human development when the pleasure principle governs. It is when the neonate need not display a wish for pleasures (need-satisfactions). They come to the infant, he said, without any volition on the infant's part, just as the fetus has had all that it wants and has nothing left to wish for. Here Ferenczi took a short but important detour from describing the state of the neonate to say, "The *childhood megalomania* of their own omnipotence is thus at least no empty delusion" (p.219). This detour led to some of his later ideas about infant fantasies or feelings of omnipotence. He returned to the main theme, that birth is visibly disagreeable to the newborn, even when oxygen privation ends:

> One gets the impression that he is far from pleased at the rude disturbance of the wish-less tranquility he had enjoyed in the womb, and indeed that *he longs to regain this situation*... The first consequence of this disturbance [and its relief by nurses] is the hallucinatory re-occupation of the satisfying situation that is missed, the untroubled existence in the warm, tranquil body of the mother... Now the curious thing is that—presupposing normal care—this hallucination is in fact realized... Since the child[3] certainly has no knowledge...of cause and effect... he must feel himself in the possession of a magical capacity that can actually realize all of his wishes by simply imagining the satisfaction of them. (*Period of magical-hallucinatory omnipotence.*) (pp.220-222)

The supposed blissful feeling of total satisfaction is soon overtaken by feelings of need. Then, as infants become aware of objects outside of their own body, they gradually learn how to use signals to attain the satisfactions of their wishes. This awareness of persons who respond to the infant, and the infant's struggles to communicate with them, lead the infant toward developing a sense of reality.

The path that Ferenczi described in earliest infancy as a *very brief* hallucinatory omnipotence was construed to be an indication of omnipotence of thought or feeling in the infant, an idea that must have been appealing to early psychoanalysts who were groping in the dark for knowledge about the beginnings of psychic structure. Thus Klein (1921), in her effort to explain how the young child tries to know the limits of his power, made use of Ferenczi's idea to assume

---

[3]*Child* was written when *infant* was meant. The same substitution appeared often in the contributions of Melanie Klein early in the 20th century, less so in the important work of Von Hug-Hellmuth (1913). The concept of infancy as an integral state had up to that time been the provinces of medicine and psychology. Freud (1905) made many references to infantile wishes or behavior, and to childhood, but not to infants or infancy. A concept of infancy as an integral period had not yet come into its own.

that a feeling of omnipotence was a regular stage in development:

> When, moved by the reality principle, [the child] attempts to make painful renunciation of his boundless omnipotent feeling, there probably arises in association with this need, so obvious in the child, of defining the limits of his own...and of parental power. (p.16)

By this surmise of a link between Ferenczi's idea of omnipotence as a stage in the development of a sense of reality and of "omnipotence feeling" in the young child, Klein changed *omnipotence of thought* to a quite different concept of *omnipotence feeling*. Searl (1929) followed Klein with references to *omnipotent fantasy*—by which she must have meant a fantasy of omnipotence.

References to infant fantasies or feelings of omnipotence have appeared through most of the 20th century. In a letter responding to Freud's remarks (1927) about religion as an illusion, Rolland wrote about a peculiar feeling that he and others had, "a sensation of 'eternity,' a feeling of something limitless, unbounded—as it were, 'oceanic'." Rolland related it to a universal religious feeling. Freud (1930) replied that he could not discover in himself this "feeling of an indissoluble bond, of being one with the world as a whole" (ibid. p.65). He preferred to consider that the infant learns gradually to differentiate the source of excitations within its own body from those that come from outside its body, and was "rather inclined to trace the 'oceanic' feeling back to an early phase of ego-feeling" (ibid. p.72), not to feelings of omnipotence. Winnicott further generalized on the idea of omnipotence, applying it to a variety of clinical and social conditions. He saw it as a manic defense (1935) probably fitting to certain psychotic conditions, as nearly a fact of experience (1953, 1967), as an antisocial tendency (1956), as an area between parent and infant (1960), and as a brief and necessary experience of the infant that may be facilitated by the mother (1962). The latter supposition may have taken on a prominence in the field because of the disarming, almost tender way that Winnicott tried to communicate his message about infant needs for gratification from the mother. It would have been more fitting to describe the state of the gratified infant as one of simple happiness rather than of omnipotence -- a concept far outside the young infant's capacity for imagining. Pumpian-Mindlin (1969) defined omnipotence as a state in which the infant cannot distinguish between the self and the external world. He called it "an initial state of unlimited objectless infantile omnipotence [which] rapidly passes...It is belied by the actual realistic helplessness of the infant" (p.214). This description of an infant's having an immense feeling of magnitude is akin to Rolland's idea about oceanic feelings in the adult.

The idea of infant omnipotence next found a place in the propositions of Mahler, Pine, and Bergman (1975) as to the existence of "an omnipotent, *autistic* orbit" in the first weeks of life (p.42). Early in the second year, the toddler experiences moods of elation, largely enforced by new locomotor ability. "...This mood often manifested itself in a quasi-delusional but age-adequate sense of grandeur, omnipotence, and conquest" (p.213); but "the repeated experiences of relative helplessness punctures the toddler's inflated sense of omnipotence" (ibid.). The gradual realization that the parents are indeed separate people means that the young child has to give up a "delusion of grandeur" as well as a belief in the omnipotence that he or she has also attributed, magically and by indirection, to the parents (ibid., p.228). This projection of omnipotence is two-edged. It suggests a capacity to satisfy the narcissistic needs of the other, that is, the infant whose needs for gratification that the parent must fulfill, and the parent whose needs for gratification that the infant must fulfill. The subject continues to be alluring. Levin (1986) rightly distinguished it from grandiosity, although like Winnicott, he saw feelings of omnipotence in the young infant as necessary for the development of mental health. Would it not be more fitting to say simply that the young infant needs to experience strong feelings of physical, emotional, and social trust (Erikson, 1945) in close objects to advance his or her mental health? Novick and Novick (1996), following Winnicott's (1953) assumption that "a child needs a long enough stage of omnipotence" [but what is long enough?] suggest the existence of a normal phase of omnipotence in which "The happy, contented infant, safe in Mother's arms and surrounded by adoring adults, is said to be in a state of infantile omnipotence, a happy delusion that he is the center of the universe with the power to make everyone meet all his needs" (pp.51-52). In fact, the young infant who has little command of his body, little or no locomotor ability, and no speech is hardly likely to feel more than a glimmering of an illusion of power, on occasions when his or her needs are smoothly met. A truer idea of an infant's feeling "great," or rather, blissful, is to be found in Lewin's (1953) exposition of the "oral triad" of wishes that may be present in the nursing infant: a wish to eat, a wish to be eaten (to enjoy a yielding relaxation), and a wish to sleep. The infant's good feeling of wishes fulfilled—assuming that the nursing or feeding has been fully comforting—vanishes almost as fast as the infant is on the way to sleep. It vanishes because for the time being it is no longer needed. Important as Ferenczi's thought about the transition from a hallucinatory omnipotence to the sense of reality may have been in its time, it presents an ideal that is attractive but not realistic. The sense of reality that most infants acquire is full of compromises. It is but a smidgen of the awareness of reality that an infant needs to develop *during infancy*. With reference to an infant's feelings of satisfaction, Freud wrote:

> One part of self-regard is primary—the residue of infantile narcissism; another part arises out of the omnipotence which is corroborated by experience (the fulfillment of *an ego ideal*) [italics added], and a third part proceeds from the satisfaction of object-libido. (1914, p.100)

Considering the psychological characteristics of sleep and waking, he also said:

> ...in speaking of our state after sleep, we say that we feel as though we were newly born. (In saying this...we are making what is probably a very false assumption about the general sensations of a newborn child, who seems likely, on the contrary, to be feeling very uncomfortable). (1916, p. 89)

In the various propositions about omnipotence in the infant, it has been missed that omnipotence belongs to a primitive mode of thinking, not an infantile experience. Studies of neurophysiological and psychological experiences of young infants may one day yield enough knowledge of their mentation to suggest that they can have a fleeting sensation of power. No such evidence yet exists. To play upon Malvolio's boast[4], the infant is neither born omnipotent, nor does he achieve omnipotence, nor should omnipotence be thrust upon him. Behind the overestimation of an infant's power lies the adult's fear of the child. Years ago Berta Bornstein (1948) wrote:

> Children frighten us by their unpredictability, their highly charged emotions, their narcissism, and by their closeness to the unconscious... although it has rarely been admitted, children throughout the ages have been considered a threat by their parents and by society in general. It is as if each older generation must prevent the rebellion of children against its cultural standards, which are jeopardized by each succeeding generation. Behind this truism, the analyst recognizes the archaic pattern of the threat of the Oedipal crime, the result of which can be found in unnecessary brutalities in training and discipline, for the alleged purpose of changing children into human beings. The opposite—extreme tolerance—constitutes a part of the same problem; it tends to placate the aggressiveness of the younger generation (pp. 695-697).

Ideas about infant omnipotence reflected a natural degree of anxiety and helplessness in understanding infant states. Unintentionally we may have disregarded an infant's vulnerability to psychological insults and his or her failure to sustain a freedom for satisfying object relatedness. Clinical histories and reports about infant behaviors and states can stir our thinking and help us construct hypotheses about factors that contribute to the generation of mental health or ill-health, but theoretical statements need to be tested systematically so that we can avoid resting on personal impressions or intriguing speculations.

---

[4]In *Twelfth Night* (Shakespeare).

Early Experience and Later Psychopathology

A number of investigators (see Kagan, 1996) have in recent years objected to a readiness in those concerned with mental health, to find connections between early experience and later psychopathology. Arlow (1981) was rightly critical of this quest for the villain in the child's past, and the accompanying tendency to see the child as a victim of parental mistakes; he stated (p.533) that unless the mother is grossly inadequate, a pathogenic influence should not be ascribed to her interaction with her child. But what shall we count as "grossly inadequate" in the complex task of mothering? There are levels of incompetence in mothers of infants that may not look inadequate or faulty, yet bear examination for what they may forewarn of difficulties that are liable to follow. Usually the primary failing is a result of parents' having had little or no education about early emotional, social, or cognitive development. Additional difficulties can occur in new parents as emotional conflicts about having taken on parental responsibilities arise, or with sadomasochistic fantasies, conscious or unconscious, about the child. Inadequacy has to be thoughtfully defined. (We have to ask: Grossly inadequate in which way? In which situation? How often? With what intensity? For what period of time? With what visible effect—immediate, proximate, distal, or cumulative?) To understand the sources of conflict with persons in the environment or within the young child, we have to take account of the gradual appearance in the infant and child of behaviors, states, and predilections that subtly may be constructing, or already have constructed a nucleus for periods of emotional distress. Early discontents that are unrelieved may propel the young child toward erecting close-to-consciousness defenses such as avoidance, externalization, restriction, and some degrees of denial. Such rudimentary self-protective methods, bred by hourly and daily habituation, can interfere with a young child's capacity to build curiosity, cognitive enjoyment and sound object relationships.

Shapiro (1981), also critical of the "march backwards" to find causative factors in infancy, asks what psychoanalysis can say about disorders that are developmental and not a sign of conflict. Much may be said. First, one does well to avoid the error contained in the mix of the concepts of developmental phase and developmental disorder. Second, child psychoanalysts can be trained to discern whether normal processes of growth are occurring, and if not, to find ways to help the young child struggle successfully with elements in his or her human environment that may be contributing to a delay or a fault in development. Third, psychoanalysis can teach us how to recognize the ways in which early conflict with elements in the external environment can lead to signs of inner conflict. And fourth, psychoanalysis can help us learn how we can turn early pathogenic conditions into the service of mental health. To disparage study of the origin of disturbance in early life is to hinder or minimize, or even preclude, our possible learning about fine differences between early conditions that are apt to induce disorder. Kagan (1996) also denies that structures formed in early stages of growth can have enduring influence. He might be correct if what he means is that long-range predictions based on single behaviors or conditions at one period in early life are of little value for uncovering sources of later mental ill health. It is commonplace to say, as Kagan does, that "infants begin life with different biologically based qualities and grow in directions that are constrained by their environments" (p.902), but he goes on to state that psychologists do not have sensitive enough methods to measure the affect states of sadness, anger, anxiety, and guilt, and so cannot prove the seminal importance of guilt and shame in motivating human behavior (p.907). Quite so, as long as the investigator has no knowledge of the ways conscious and unconscious ideas and affects can structure behavior and development proceeding from earliest childhood. Lewis (1997), along similar lines, argues that the early mother-infant relationship has little or no significance for the child's later social adjustment, and that too much importance is placed on the first one or two years of life. He is right only if one makes predictions of specific forms of social behavior without consideration of the context in which they appeared originally, and in which they are or are not observable years later. Valid connections are to be found only in intensive direct observations of sample-clusters of emotional and cognitive experiences of the infant and child that recur day after day, week after week, and month after month, in the child's first years.

These could permit short-term predictions at intervals of weeks and of months in the first year, and gradually longer intervals during the next two to four years. This would make for a complex research program, but it could yield unique information about specific sources of psychopathology that appear in the first two to three years of life.

Anthropological investigations of infant-rearing have repeatedly shown significant relations between modes of infant and child care and children's socialization. The first large cross-cultural study in this area (Whiting, 1963) explored relations between different patterns of early child-rearing and the differences in personality and ways of perceiving the surrounding world that follow from them. For a psychoanalytic view of connections between infant care and later behaviors, we may look back to Erikson's studies (1950), aided by the investigations of Kroeber (1925), and Mekeel (1932), of the infant and child-rearing customs in two American Indian tribes early in the 20th century, the Sioux in the Northern Plains, and the Yurok on the West coast. The traditions of the two tribes were distinctly different from each other and from our culture. These studies dramatize important associations between infantile experience and later propensities for anxiety and conflict, or for freedom of thought and action.

The Developmental Approach

Information about experiential events that have slow and silent influence on an infant's well-being is still meager, although, as indicated above, the gap has been narrowed since approximately the mid-20th century. Research findings have also come from developmental psychologists[5] and psychoanalysts[6] but the latter field is too young to have developed methods applicable to young infants, children and adolescents whose behaviors have not been subject to psychoanalytic research. We have no systematic studies,

---

[5]Emde (1983), Emde, Gaensbauer & Harmon (1976); Stern (1985, 1988); Talberg, Cuoto Rosa, & O'Donnell (1988), and Trevarthan (1979).

[6]Brody (1980, 1982), Brody & Axelrad (1970, 1978); Brody & Siegel (1992); Call (1964, 1968, 1980); Nachman (1991, 1998), Spitz (1945, 1946a, 1946b).

for example, of normal psychological concomitants of weaning[7], teething, being left alone or crying for long periods; of the effects of excessive reliance on pacifiers and transitional objects, both promoted by misunderstandings of oral needs of infants and young children (see Brody, 1980); of methods of toilet training and of sexual education; or of feelings related to loss of object love within the family. Issues like these, with which parents are confronted over and over again, are usually brought to pediatricians, who until the last few decades may have had little education about the social and emotional needs of infants. Important exceptions lie in the work of Ribble (1943), Spock (1945), and Leach (1977).

A little history may help to explain the diminishing interest in instinctual dynamics during infancy and early childhood. In the years after Freud (1923) formulated the structural theory and ego development took center stage in psychoanalysis, leaving instinct theory in the wings, it appeared to Hartmann (1939) that knowledge about normal adaptation was needed to advance basic psychoanalytic theory. He had in mind the body of emerging knowledge about psychological growth in the first years of life, as shown in the work of the psychologists Karl Buhler (1919) and Charlotte Buhler (1935) and in the concept of the "average expectable environment" expressed by the sociologist Max Weber (1921). For Weber the concept was meant to account for the network of usual events which, if known—the prerequisite is that they are knowable—permit the individual to make rational decisions. But when Hartmann referred to the average expectable environment, he was looking for a way to render psychoanalysis into a general psychology that did not have the instinctual drives and the dynamic unconscious as its major principles. To explain the process of adaptation he proposed that certain ego functions (meaning functions controlled by the ego) are independent of the drives and depend rather on "inborn apparatuses" that become operative with development and maturation. He also placed great store on the existence of "conflict-

---

[7]A partial exception appeared in a discussion of weaning by M. Klein (1936). Her statements about the gradualness with which weaning should be accomplished were well taken, and so were her observations of infant behavior (1952). Both suggest that had she written more about actual infant behaviors and feelings, and not given way to categorical statements about their aggressive and destructive fantasies, her theoretical influence might have been more positive.

free spheres" of development that allowed for primary and secondary autonomy during early development (1939, Chap. 9; 1952, pp. 16-20; see also Brody, 1956, pp. 359-361). These emphases by Hartmann may have had an undeclared purpose of repudiating the claims of Klein (1928, 1930) that persecutory and depressive fantasies dominated in the life of the young infant. But Hartmann's thesis, to enclose normal maturation and conflict-free development within the psychoanalytic framework, has so far lost ground.

The quick appreciation by many psychoanalysts of Hartmann's assignment of priority to adaptive forces in the ego led in following years to an attenuation of fundamental psychoanalytic concepts concerning the development of psychic structure. For some, the increased attention to the ways of the ego may have brought a relief from the murkier subjects of instinctual drives and infantile sexuality. This drift towards ego theory, driven by a variety of factors, has contributed, I think, to the present abundance of relational theories (Richards, Bachant, & Lynch, 1995). A. Freud and Burlingham (1943), observing the plight of infants in war nurseries, considered that the infants' disturbances were a result of separations from their mothers after the age of five or six months. As they gave no count of how many infants were observed before or after those months, their statements did not arouse attention to the more general effects of early or temporary absence of the mother. Soon after, Spitz (1945) described the costs of emotional deprivation among infants who were institutionalized for periods during their first year of life. They suffered from "hospitalism" (1945) often with lethal results (1946a), and from "anaclitic depression" (1946b). Then Bowlby (1960) addressed the plight of infants separated from home and family for days or weeks. He named their stressful condition "separation anxiety," a name that has gradually become a diagnostic category referring to many kinds of breaks in continuity in relationships, at all ages. In the current literature of infant and child mental health, separation anxiety appears to have supplanted the more intense fear of object loss (perhaps because separation is a more palatable idea than object loss), and the more crucial fear of abandonment, which implies hostility in the (abandoning) parent. Provence and Lipton (1962) were among the first to bring confirmation of Spitz's principal theses about the dire effects of institutionalization on infant development. Emotional neglect among infants reared at home but not socioeconomically deprived was not yet a matter of study, even among advanced professional students of mental health.

At the beginning of the Nazi regime in 1933, analysts had begun to apply analytic principles to childhood. The first few papers on "child analysis" appeared in the German *Zeitschrift fur Psychoanalyse Pedagogik* in the early 1930's. They included papers from B. Bornstein and her sister, S. Bornstein, Geleerd, and Greig. Early in that decade, analysts trained by Freud or his disciples came from Germany, Czechoslovakia, Hungary, and France to New York, Boston, and Philadelphia. Ernst Kris, Heinz Hartmann, and Anna Freud then pioneered a new publication, *The Psychoanalytic Study of the Child*, published annually in New York since 1945. During its first decade, the book contained a number of fine papers describing child psychoanalysis and related problems. Those case histories began to diminish in the 1950's; increasingly, the volume contained papers on such subjects as "problems with normal and pathological development," "clinical contributions," "applied psychoanalysis," and varieties of "clinical and research problems" rather than child analysis. Papers on child analytic treatment have gradually decreased; by the 1990's, there were fewer contributions about clinical problems, but more on child development, theory, application of psychoanalysis, and reports of research. Contributions about child analysis proper have diminished, and in the last few years, have hardly appeared. This has been a result of the many practical difficulties involved in making analysis available to children. The economic constraints that hinder parents from bringing children to regular sessions (originally 4-5 times a week), or even weekly sessions, have increased significantly (especially since nowadays both parents are more likely to be employed full-time). Additionally, the training of child analysts has become protracted and highly expensive; as a result, many clinicians often assume that child analysis is outmoded or unnecessary. Another factor in this decline of child analysis is the increasing incursion of many other "therapies" (Kleinian, Adlerian, Rogerian etc). An unfortunate result is the impoverishment of the clinical and theoretical understanding of problems of childhood and adolescence. A major interference with the proper understanding of children's conflicts has been a rapid rise in the medication of children to help parents deal with the children's emotional problems. It is now common for parents to think of children as being hyperactive, depressed, or affected by attention deficit disorder, rather than unhappy. Even taking into account the help of social workers, educated teachers, and a variety of medical and psychological specialists to whom they may have access, parents are essentially on their own in identifying and addressing their children's difficulties.

During recent years psychologists have emphasized the importance of attachment for the infant, a concept that grew out of Bowlby's interest in ethological studies, especially the work of Lorenz (1966), which led him to formulate ideas about what he called component instinctual responses that bind mother and infant. (The behaviors he named were crying, smiling, following, sucking and clinging; these behaviors have no connection to the component instincts described by Freud [1905].) Bowlby saw clinging and following as more important for attachment than sucking and crying. In this, he was much influenced by Ainsworth's studies of mother-infant interaction. Bowlby defined "attachment behavior as behavior that has proximity to an attachment figure as a predictable outcome and whose evolutionary function is protection of the infant from danger; that the attachment has its own motivation." Here attachment refers to behavior, rather than to the inner experience of the child; it refers to affective connections between persons but does not in itself stipulate the meaning or the quality of those connections. The concept of attachment omits reference to the libidinal and aggressive instinctual forces connecting mother and infant.

With the passage of time, as the negative effects of gross maternal deprivation have become better known (Weil, 1992), other concerns about infant growth in normal home settings have come to the fore, and there have been more published studies about the neurological development of normal infants. Statements about growth in a variety of areas are often classified as developmental—sometimes meaning phase-specific—often with a tacit expectation that the behaviors will pass because children change as they grow, although behavior of a young child that is called developmental may lie barely within normal limits, like a passing academic grade of 65 or 70. "Developmental" is an over-valued adjective; it lends itself to indistinct meanings; often it appears to have replaced a former inclination to assess a child's behavior as "part of a phase." (I believe that the term, "developmental approach," first appeared in Hartmann's discussion of the mutual influences of the ego and the id (1952, p.16).) These developmental explanations reduce emphasis on instinctual drive theory. Arlow (1981) correctly noted that a dependence on the developmental approach "minimizes the element of conflict in favor of developmental deficit" (p.511). References to developmental aspects of human behavior are of course implicit in many fields that study human behavior, in conjunction with the allied notions of periods, outcomes, processes, transitions, advances, disorders, and so on.

"Developmental" was highlighted with specific reference to children when Anna Freud (1965) presented her assessment of "developmental lines" to describe the stages through which infants and children gradually build control of their ego functions. She provided an outline of how development, seen psychoanalytically, proceeds in a variety of areas. The lines did not include a comparable outline of the vast number of interferences with development that could be addressed, and so the "lines" have left an impression among many educators that development is a much smoother or more ideal process than it often is. This surely was not A. Freud's intention. Her wish was to delineate frames of reference by which to describe paths of normal ego development in childhood. I am inclined to believe that the popular appeal of the developmental approach has in part reflected an over-eager response to her concept of developmental lines, as it coalesced with Hartmann's then current propositions about adaptation[8]. This response has led to generalizations that obscure differences in kinds and levels of development; the specificity and significance of particular behaviors is diluted or lost when they are, as it were, tossed into a hopper assigned to "the developmental." Loeb (1982) wrote of generalization as a defense that may be likened to intellectualization, and frequently combines with other

---

[8]Mayes (1994) has provided a fine appraisal of Hartmann's position.

defenses, such as isolation[9]. "Developmental" allows for premature generalization; it incorporates a range of unspecified conditions. It is comparable to a loose reliance on "constitutional." It makes for confusion between developmental psychology, which is concerned with motor, physical, cognitive, emotional, and social growth; and psychopathology, which is concerned with mental conflict.

When in 1967 Sidney Axelrad and I told A. Freud of our surprise about the high frequency of signs of unfavorable development in our (normal) infant sample (n=131), she quickly minimized their significance as being just "matters of personality." We supposed this was because her primary interest was in the infantile neurosis. In numerous contexts during the next years, she reiterated her opinion that the roots of personality, personality structure (1970a, p.162), and personal attributes (1970b, pp. 193-197), did not belong in the same sphere as neurosis. She was emphatic in her opinion that the linking of neurotic symptoms to the earliest events in the infant's first year of life was a serious error (1974, p. 71). I believe it was correct not to speak of neurosis in the infant, but it would have been more correct to note the inception of psychological problems among infants that, unheeded, proceed within the very next years to the formation of barely conscious infantile conflict. A. Freud, like her father, had so much to contribute about neurotic conflict arising in early childhood that it was perhaps natural for them to skip over the first two to three years of life. This error came to the surface in separating out the developmental disturbances in the first years of life as reflections of personality. Personality becomes known in a social setting; it defines how a person is seen by others. It does not refer to a person's inner experience. Attributing behavior in the preoedipal period to personality, or to a developmental phase, hampers recognition of infantile behaviors that may be incurring psychological disorder. A simple example is low frustration tolerance, or a poor capacity to bear tension. For if that low tolerance moves toward chronic demandingness, or loss of temper, or moods of sullen anger or sad retreat, it is no longer

---

[9]"Generalization," he said, "is the opposite of isolation, in that in isolation the connections between thoughts and affects or between thoughts and thoughts are severed, whereas in generalization, such connections are multiplied" (pp. 417-418).

a matter of personality but of a character dimension. Personality "refers to aspects of a person that are open to view. It transpires in social settings...Character [in contrast] refers to the internal quality of a person" (Brody and Siegel, 1992, pp. 3-5). Naturally, when the poor tolerance of frustration and related behaviors and affects are relieved in good time, development can proceed to an advancing of the child's capacity to develop an observing ego. Then he or she can see the need to settle partially internalized conflicts with mother and father, and to reduce fears of losing parental love. It is interesting to find that although A. Freud's knowledge of what children need from their mothers was keen, she (1954) maintained that a mother can influence a child's development but cannot produce neurosis[10]. No doubt, in her effort to make utterly clear that the infantile neurosis is essentially a resultant of the child's internalized conflict, she set aside the powerful influence of a mother on her child's mental health. Abrams (1990) aptly discussed "developmental" as a term that fosters no end of ambiguities, and "compromises the study of the actual developmental process" (p.650).

Signs of rising conflict can be seen in the latter months of the infant's first year, if not before, in behaviors such as longing, jealousy, shame, rage, and disgust. These behaviors rise markedly in the child's second year, along with his or her object representations. They are visible in abundance during the young child's progress from acting on impulse to thoughtful action. Suzy is an envious little girl of two. When she admires her friend's new doll, does she ask to hold it, or quickly announce that she is going to get one just like it on her birthday, or does she grab it in spite of its owner's protests? Is she manifesting jealousy, or anger, or fright that she has no such doll to show? We should like to know if and when these emotions can change. When a friend suddenly trips and has a bad fall on the street, does Suzy rush to comfort her, or turn to her mother for help, or look bewildered, or cry, or stand still, too appalled to move? Whatever she does probably reflects the capacity she has so far developed for empathy, or for a readiness to feel helpless, or

---

[10]A reading of Young-Bruehl's "Looking for Anna Freud's Mother" (1989) suggests to me that this statement represented a reaction-formation against a devaluation of her own mother, and so an excessive need to exonerate mothers in general.

perhaps for a self-centered turning away to busy herself elsewhere. How her immediate behavior is responded to by the adult in charge, and whether that behavior can be improved tactfully, reveal her present capacity to exercise judgment. That is to say, her behavior will give some indication of her ego maturity, and so of her being on the way to building a base for superego health.

One might say that a sublimation of the component instincts, side by side with a forward development of the major instinctual drives, can contribute to the building of a capstone for the institution of the superego. At present we have only scattered information, mostly in clinical reports, about the expression of the component instincts. A. Freud referred to their connection to personal attributes and character formation as "preparing the way for regressions... and as true forerunners of the infantile neurosis proper" (1970b, p. 197), a connection that was dimmed by her stress on developmental issues. Whether the component instincts are acted upon, or held back, or serve an early form of sublimation, they generate personal qualities that can flourish before as well as during and after the oedipal phase, as may be seen in the young child's normally rising struggles with parents and siblings for preference, praise, favors, love, and power. Study of their emergence, intensity, and duration in the infantile period should reveal much about the momentum they can provide for the development of sound object-relatedness and character formation. Longitudinal observations beginning in early infancy could help us to sort out differences among those component instinctual behaviors that are ephemeral, those that nourish normal and positive qualities, and those that give shelter to neurotic or character disorders or perversions. Psychopathology is also developmental.

The psychological life of the infant or toddler with their only partial mastery of language and motility is within the province of psychoanalysis because these incomplete masteries are interlarded with the development of object relations. An ideal method of studying early experiences lies first of all in direct observations of the range and quality of the infant's body language. Disorders *in statu nascendi* are easy to miss by too readily assuming that since they belong to a phase of development they do not indicate conflict; this assumption is often made, particularly when an infant's condition does not have immediate meaning to parents or other caregivers because they have never been educated to the ways of infant and child growth, or when new information about even a small part of the infant's behavior that deserves watching is perceived by them as a threat to their parental sophistication. The old rationalization that the infant or child "will grow out of it," is still too much with us. According to my studies of infants and their mothers, and of children with both parents, I have had reason to hypothesize that character formation develops from the vicissitudes of pregenital drive derivatives, and from the events from latency to puberty. We may hope that investigators with more data and finer methods of analyzing the intricacies of early psychological need-fulfillment may be able to test this thesis.

THE COMPONENT
INSTINCTS

2

The Component Instincts

Freud's propositions (1905) about libido and aggression as the two biological instincts have been supported by a long line of studies of psychological conditions during infancy, childhood, and adolescence. Early childhood is understood to encompass events that transpire from the close of infancy, at about fifteen months, to about the end of the third year, that period always dependent on the social and psychological conditions in which the normal infant has been reared. By then, in a sustaining environment, the young child's basic locomotor and verbal abilities have usually been achieved, the intensity of preoccupations about his or her body functions has dimmed, as have elementary concerns about differences between male and female bodies. In the next two to three years, the child's raw instinctual wishes and fantasies press forward; the child is about to enter the so-called phallic phase[11].

11This designation would seem to affirm the young child's idea that the phallus is the sexual organ of both sexes; as we nowhere find reference to a "clitoral phase," we seem to affirm the common assumption of children that girls have no organ to match the penis. A more fitting name for the female part comparable to the phallic phase would be vulvar. While there is no study, as far as I have found, of when or under what conditions girls discover their vulva or their clitoris, I have observed masturbatory pleasure among female infants in the second half of their first year; but for many months

During the third quarter of the infant's first year, derivatives of the two main instinctual drives begin to appear in behaviors such as gladness, sadness, longing, jealousy, pride, shame, and rage. These affects and their related impulses increase markedly in the child's second year, usually in accordance with the spread and quality of his or her object representations. They may readily be seen during the young child's progress from acting on impulse to thoughtful action and to the building of frustration tolerance.

In his original discussion Freud named three component instincts: voyeurism, exhibitionism, and cruelty, referred to by Fenichel (1945) as partial instincts. Unlike the biologically rooted instincts of libido and aggression; the components are understood to be determined by a person's relations to (living) objects. In his original discussion of these instincts Freud (1905) would seem to have argued backward, so to speak, from the pathological to the normal: from voyeurism to the normal aims of looking (searching, investigating), from exhibitionism to the normal wish to be looked at, and from cruelty to kindness. Abraham (1908) described these three pairs of component instincts as representing active and passive counterparts of each other:

> One impels the individual to dominate his sexual object, the other to submit to its will. Feelings of pity and horror, for example, originate from the sublimation of these tendencies. If sublimation [of the wish for mastery] does not take place it is likely to engender the perversions called *sadism* and *masochism* respectively. (p. 83)

The work of the component instincts is easily observable in the behavior of young children as they normally give way to impulses so much more freely than they do in later years. The third component, cruelty, appears to be less natural; it is usually less open to view than voyeurism and exhibitionism, and starker in appearance. I follow Hanly's suggestion (1978) that hostile affects rather then a basic

---

the girl may assume that the opening between her thighs has only one use, a place to let out urine. Freud (Footnote #2, 1905) described the final pregenital phase as "phallic" (p. 199). In this he followed Abraham (1924) who described the phase as having "a biological prototype in the embryo's undifferentiated genital disposition, which is the same for both sexes."

impulse toward cruel actions constitutes the base for aggressive acts. The interplay of cruelty with sadism and masochism would seem obvious, yet its contributions to early childhood development have received spare notice. It has been discussed mainly by A. Freud (1945), who outlined the meaning of the component instincts (but cited no data about their onset and duration or about their contribution to ego and character development) and also by Compton (1981). Moore and Fine (1990) referred to them, in the context of the psychoanalytic treatment of adolescents and adults, mainly for their influence on foreplay, perversions, and sublimations, as learned from psychoanalytic treatment of adolescents and adults. Few data have appeared, however, as to when and how those component instincts gain prominence during the preoedipal phases and how they may remain powerful forces in subsequent years. This paucity of observations is probably related to the overriding interest, through most of the twentieth century, in the vicissitudes of the Oedipus complex; in other words, the psychoanalytic literature has been more devoted to the main instincts of libido, with its sources in the erotogenic zones of the body, and of aggression, with its sources in the musculature (Abraham 1908; Hanly 1978). The psychological events that take place beside those main developments have by and large remained outside the range of clinical notice.

Freud (1905) indicated that while the two major instincts have their sources in the body, the component instincts have their sources in other persons experienced as objects (p. 192); they involve the skin, the eyes, and the nose, as the earliest erogenous zones that satisfy instinctual aims (pp.179-185). Described positively, there is first the infant's experience of the whole body's being held, bathed, cleaned, carried, fed, and being placed in a variety of positions, or of being allowed to move the body or its parts or to lie still. Within hours of birth the neonate can feel pleasure in responding to sensory stimuli; within days he or she can enjoy continuous repetitions of those experiences. The passive experience of being touched arouses the complementary desire to touch, being looked at arouses the complementary desire to look, being talked or sung to arouses responsive vocalizations, and all of these pleasures stir wishes for their repetition, along with a psychological alertness to things and events in the near environment. A young infant who is thriving can respond to external stimuli with a medley of positive excitements visible in head and body movements and vocalizations. By five or six months he or she can enjoy showing "tricks" with mouth, chin, and eyes. Some young infants develop a pleased searching gaze, enjoy watching moving objects and anticipating events in the very near environment. When such pleasures are experienced comfortably, one may be able to see an outgoing attitude toward human objects. These behaviors are understood to have their onset in the oral phase, and to gain consistency during the period of learning to move limbs, to handle objects, to push, toss, and carry them, so to take charge of their intimate worlds. Within a few months the toddler discovers, with help usually from an intimate person, that he or she can cover space by walking, running, jumping, and climbing; and to utter words, cry out, or shout when it pleases him, and all these accomplishments are far more exciting than the young infant has the means to express. Tasks of the toddler that require self-care become routines that can bring the glory of independent action, or of choosing to be silent, or still, or reflective, or negative and rejecting. All of these behaviors contain dramatic possibilities. They demand active practice, with myriad little but important variations, from the young child's point of view. On the other hand, infants who are left alone, unaddressed or left in discomfort for hours at a time, usually learn to avert their gaze or to avoid looking and listening, as if they have become impervious to external stimuli. Or they may steer away from those social encounters or from exploration of objects in the near environment that bring no immediate pleasure.

During the first months of life the infant acquires an awareness of his or her lower body parts because they are so often examined and cleaned by the caregiver. Months before the infant can have thoughtful recognition of the acts of urination and defecation, he or she can feel pleasure in pushing out a fecal mass or holding it in, and can enjoy the warm wetness in his or her lower body. Buoyed up by these new-found anal and urinary capacities, toddlers experience a degree of autonomous control of their lower body parts, and of some persons or things. The pleasure that is first derived from erogenous and sensory parts now comes to include muscles and limbs. The way ahead may be uneven emotionally, as so much of the child's experience depends on the quality of environmental care available, and on his or her freedom to employ the new-found power to say no, in action or inaction. Physical and cognitive capacities emerge so rapidly and so variously in the infant's second year that adults often are astonished at the toddler's new capacities which seem to have appeared quite suddenly. There is much for the young toddler to do in order to feel in charge of his or her body; so much to look at and to reach for; so many ways to make sounds, noises, and words; to watch and imitate another child; to hold, carry, or fling away objects; to test the quality of things to smell and taste. All of the healthy toddler's senses are on the alert, and he responds gladly to any acknowledgment of his new-found capacities, although soon enough his caregiver demands control of the dark smelly soft stuff that comes out of a foreign place in the child's lower back. Praised for letting out the fecal mass, the toddler feels proud; missing that verbal reward, he is likely to feel uncomfortably alone, with a vague want of approval or reassurance regarding the command of his lower body. As in the latter part of the toddler's second year his physical and cognitive capacities grow fast, both child and parent may be confronted with troubling emotional tasks. Each now has to consider the other's expectations, and each must learn to accommodate to unexpected limits to freedom.

With reference to the body parts that serve the biological instincts, Freud described the erogenous zones of the body, the lips and mouth, the anus and the genitalia. The component instincts stem, however, from relationships to persons. They govern active and passive wishes to look at or to be looked at, and unless gradually sublimated, they facilitate voyeurism and exhibitionism, and in some cases, the development of the perversions. Freud did not identify which body parts subserve cruelty, although he referred to its instinctual basis in the drive to master.

> The cruelty component of the sexual instinct develops in childhood even more independently of the sexual activities that are attached to the erotogenic zones. Cruelty in general comes easily to the childish nature, since the obstacle that brings the instinct for

mastery to a halt at another person's pain—namely a capacity for pity—is developed relatively late....It may be assumed that the impulse of cruelty arises from the instinct for mastery and appears at a period of sexual life at which the genitals have not yet taken over their later role. It then dominates a phase of sexual life which we shall later describe as a pregenital organization.... The absence of the barrier of pity brings with it a danger that the connection between the cruel and the erotogenic instincts... may prove unbreakable in later life... At about the same time as the sexual life of children reaches its first peak, between the ages three and five, they also begin to show signs of the activity which may be ascribed to the instinct for knowledge or research. (1905, p.192-194).

But the origins of the instinct for cruelty, like the origins of the scopophilic instinct, Freud wrote, "were not yet completely intelligible," adding:

We have already discovered in examining the erotogenic zones that...certain regions of the skin merely show a special intensification of a kind of susceptibility to stimulus which is possessed to a certain degree by the whole cutaneous surface. We shall therefore not be surprised to find that very definite erotogenic effects are to be ascribed to certain kinds of general stimulation of the skin. (p. 201)

Here it is the "whole cutaneous surface" covering the muscles and nerves rather than the erogenous parts that form the biological source of passive and active satisfactions in cruel acts. This seems to mean that the cruel acts are emboldened not by the skin, but by impulses that govern the muscles and nerves inside the enclosing skin. The impulses are driven to hurt the object of the child's anger, or to denigrate that object in some way. The impulse to hurt the enemy is enacted with the use of assaults. Billy has just picked up the little red car that Tim has been looking for; Tim, with a yell and a kick tries to grab the car back; so Billy knocks down the garage that Tim built for it; each boy tingles with excitement and pleasure in "getting even;" Tim is aroused by the pain and humiliation heaped on him; he kicks Billy's leg and pushes him away. Arms, legs, shoulders, and hateful looks take part in this angry encounter. Even an infant of nine or ten months, feeling slighted or physically hurt in any way, can hit, push, or pinch, arousing simultaneous excitement in his offender and in himself.

Most references to the component instincts have veered toward the pathological, without recognition of their positive aspects: i.e., the desire to look for the purpose of learning and communicating (rather than to be a voyeur); the desire to be looked at, as found in sublimations in the creative arts and the humanities (rather than to be an exhibitionist); and the desire to be kind and compassionate (rather than to be cruel). Cruelty, the third component instinct explicated by Freud, is more difficult to comprehend as instinctual than are voyeurism and exhibitionism, because in them the function of the eye is clear. Freud had less to say about the erotogenic source of cruelty in the body, but almost any part of the whole body, especially the limbs, may serve in its execution. Cruelty contains a more intense degree of the drive to master or to subdue an object than do the first two component instincts. It is expressed in offensive words or acts, and it intrudes harshly upon another's mind or body or on one's own. Among children, the angry word or act may appear without warning—in an impudent grab of another's possession, or a sudden yank of a girl's long hair, actions too good to miss! Outdoors, five-year-old Annie is watching over her year-old baby sister who is trying to walk on the pavement; their 18-month-old cousin Meg, who has joined them, suddenly stops for a bare moment—just long enough for her to grasp the baby's shoulder and push her to the ground; Annie remonstrates, whereupon Meg sticks out her tongue in disdain, and goes proudly on her way; a little later, at a safe distance, Meg repeats her rude performance, and if no watching adult interferes, her taunting can become cruel. Such bare hostile acts may be seen in an impudent push of a classmate off a favorite seat, or a yank of her dress; even a one-year-old can angrily pinch, scratch, push, or bite. Such acts represent an active wish to subjugate another person, often also to watch the victim's reaction to the sudden assault. The obverse inner masochistic wish to be subjugated or to receive pain stoically may be hardly conscious and may seem motiveless except when it is enacted in imaginative play, as when pretending to be the victim of an angry parent, or a mean teacher, or a harsh policeman.

Children are enthralled when they happen to witness punishments of other children in the form of criticism, reproaches, isolations, or physical assaults. Parental threats to spank are in these days less commonly expressed than they were decades ago, especially in families who have been educated about its deplorable effects. In the course of the 20th century, physical punishments have lost credit in most schools in the United States and abroad. Newspaper cartoons and comic strips with themes of cruel punishments have long lost prominence. In Germany we once had Strewwelpeter[12] (Slovenly Peter), the willful boy who would not stop sucking his thumb (noted by Freud, 1905, fn. p. 179) so that both his thumbs had to be cut off; or the girl who did not mind her mother's warnings against playing with matches, so that she was burned to death; and more dire warnings to children who did not listen to adults' admonitions against disobedience or waywardness. Of the 12 misbehaving children depicted in the latter book, one was a girl, Pauline—her name derived from that of a boy—and all the others were boys, the wickedness of boys and the innocence of girls seeming to have been taken for granted.

Freud (1908) described typical attitudes that emerge when use of the toilet becomes a major accomplishment in the young child's life: *orderliness*, *obstinacy*, and *frugality* become token modes of behavior. These attitudes, which usually come into their prime in the latter part of the child's second year, may dominate his or her behavior well into their third year. Rules, routines, and the pleasures of task-completion that were beyond the toddler's imagination just a few months ago are now to be valued. Under pleasing conditions the young child acquires a capacity to feel pride in this efficiency. Under displeasing conditions, his or her negative impulsivity may become intense: "Go 'way!" "S'op!" During this period in which

---

[12]A slim book by Heinrich Hoffman, dramatically illustrated (Bruceerick Ungar Publishing Company, 105 East 24th Street, New York, NY, 1845). It is also noted in Smithsonian Collection of Newspaper Comics (Blackhood & Williams, 1977).

parent and child differ, more or less vehemently, as to how to respond to the pressing demands of the body, the adult may notice growth in the child toward an observing ego (Brody,1990)[13], and toward aspirations to accomplish new tasks; or at the other extreme, the child may turn to negativistic responses, a surrender of aspirations, and a regression to infantile wishes and fears. A peremptory assertion of power takes over all other needs: "Outa my way!" "Dat's mine!" A silent hard push or a proud yell declare triumph—or an absolute right, whatever may immediately be won. This was the state of the not quite-three-year-old hyperactive patient who demanded that I tell her at once if I had a husband; soon she accosted any man whom she happened to see enter my office building to ask his name; or she brightly greeted another man, saying excitedly, "Hi, husband!" One of her favorite activities in my office was to jump on the couch rapidly and repeatedly, each time saying loudly, "Look't! Look't!" Questions eventually led her to explain, as she kept her eyes on me, "Look at me! Look at me!" She was here being the exhibitionist—and also the voyeur as she kept her eyes on me—and I was to be the voyeur. At the moment, the twin component wishes to look at and to be looked at dominated her being.

In the United States, at the turn of the century, we had the *Katzenyammer Kids*, Hans and Fritz (1919)[14], whose everyday misbehaviors led them to be placed side by side across their father's knees and vigorously spanked, each comic strip ending with vivid pictures of the screaming boys. Occasionally there was a happier ending, as when the boys played out their Vildvester[15] stories of heroism in a struggle against nasty adults. Opposites of cruelty in children are to be seen in their acts of tenderness, sympathy, or friendliness, however small. Soft overtures or responses like these are seen when the baby offers a bit of food to mother, with a proud

---

[13]The Observing Ego, Presented in an award by the New York State Psychological Association, 1990. Unpublished.

[14]Originally appeared in The American Examiner, 1911. See the Smithsonian Collection of Newspaper Comics, ed. B. Blackhead & M. Williams, The Smithsonian Institution Press & Harry N. Abrams, Inc. 1977, Opp. 27, 28; and note p. 19: Hans and Fritz, originally the two schrecklich kinder of Wilhelm Busch's *Max and Moritz* (1865).

[15]Notably portrayed in the years of war between the United States and Germany (1914-1917).

smile; places a hand gently on the hand of another child, as if offering some kind of kinship; squeals with joy when an older sibling makes funny sounds. Reaction-formations against cruelty may be enacted at any age under normal conditions of thoughtfulness; and as indicated above, during sublimations of instinctual drives.

The appearance of the component instinctual behaviors during the child's first years has received little attention. Their importance in the young child's life appears to have been bypassed, although they may be seen everyday and everywhere, for good or ill, among young children who are awake and active. I am referring to the ways they later express the instinctual active and passive wishes to look at and to be looked at (voyeurism and exhibitionism) and to give or to be subjected to pain (cruelty). As Freud indicated, the component instincts relinquish their influence and become subdued in the latency period, but continue to play a subsidiary part in adult sexuality. During the phallic phase certain important alterations appear in the sexual attitudes, wishes, and behaviors of children. Boys are likely to exhibit pride in the penis and what it can do in states of erection and urination; girls, more or less envious of those unique powers, often try to urinate in a standing position; and some boys who express wishes to be girls find ways to hide their penis between their thighs. The message given to girls, that only they have a capacity to some day have a baby grow inside their bellies is barely palliative—it takes so long for that baby to come, some time in the far unknowable future. For both boys and girls, interest in the mysteries of birth and death increase as they move into the oedipal phase, and decrease under the rising influence of superego strictures in the latency period.

During latency one may usually observe a rise in the child's self-esteem as he or she learns to abide by rules, to acquire skills and knowledge, to broaden and strengthen object relations (playmates, friends) and to enjoy a capacity for sustained physical or mental activity. On the negative side, we may see rebelliousness, regressions, symptomatic disorders, many forms of anxiety, and surrender of aims toward mature object relations and achievements. As the preoccupations of the latency period wane, the child's instinctual impulses become less evident than before. A middle age of childhood sets in, from about the tenth year to prepuberty. It is heralded by physical and psychological signs of body change, which for a time prepare the child for the passage into preadolescence. The absence of systematic study of the component instincts is probably in large part a result of overarching conceptualizations about the Oedipus complex, which has been in the limelight of psychoanalytic theory from its beginnings. In general, as indicated above, there has been a failure of opportunities to make systematic direct observations of changing psychological behaviors of children from birth to about age four, behaviors largely unrelated to oedipal wishes or conflicts, during the prephallic, phallic, and preoedipal years.

Therefore I present data from a longitudinal research study of infants, children, and adolescents (Brody, 1970; Brody and Axelrad, 1978; Brody and Siegel, 1992) that illustrate the presence of the component instincts as they affected the emotional, social, and intellectual development of five subjects observed in the study. As reported before (Brody & Siegel, 1992), all of the infant subjects were observed at regular intervals in their first year of life (n=131), annually from ages four through seven (n=121), and at age 18 (n=91); 15 younger siblings of the original group were also observed at ages two and/or three as well. From this mass of data I have selected five subjects to describe the observations of component instinctual behaviors. I have chosen the five from among those observed at ages two and/or three (previously, we had only seen them through age one, then again annually at ages 4-7). I am indebted to the mothers who agreed to participate in the research project before and after the birth of their infants, by visiting our offices at stated intervals to report about their maternal experiences with the given infant and child and to allow their children to receive psychological tests, at the same intervals; I am equally indebted to those fathers of the child subjects who were willing and able to be interviewed about their experiences with their children and their views about child-rearing.

The mothers and fathers were told that they were doing us a service by helping us learn about the experiences of infants with their parents and that we would not provide advice about problems that might arise in our study of the children.

THE SUBJECTS

3
The Subjects

The data in the following section are intended to bring forward only direct observations of the children's development of *voyeurism*, *exhibitionism*, and *cruelty*, or their opposites, from birth to age seven and again at age eighteen. Therefore I have omitted most references to their feeding and toilet training histories, and their passing health or behavior problems, unless they have clearly impinged, for better or worse, on the development of each child's component instincts. I have added a few remarks about the child's familial environment and the quality of child care received insofar as they affected the child's psychological growth. For the sake of clarity about the social environment in which each of the five children lived, I note each child's birth order in the family (BO), the family's socioeconomic status (SES), the appearance and behavior of the mother (M), and where available of the father (F), and statements about the child drawn from our interviews[16] by E (examiner, who usually also carried out the infant's or child's psychological tests[17]) with M

[16]For a detailed account of the interview form, please refer to Appendix B.
[17]For a more detailed account of the tests administered, please refer to Appendix A.

and separately with F, about their parental attitudes and activities. Information noted by O (observer) during in-school observations of the children is also included in this section. At ages 4, 5, and 18, all of the subjects were asked to make drawings. Four year olds were prompted with blank paper and crayons, at which point the examiner would wait and observe to see if the child would create a drawing spontaneously. Then, the child would be asked to draw a man. At age five the procedure changes slightly: children were again given the opportunity to draw spontaneously, then afterwards asked to draw a person (many of the children needed help to understand the meaning of the word 'person'). Next, the five year olds were requested to draw their family. Eighteen year olds were asked to draw a person, then a person of the opposite sex. Then they were presented with the optional choice of drawing their family doing something together, and many declined. All of the interviews at age eighteen were carried out by me.

To be included in the study, all of the infants and children were reported by their pediatricians to be physically normal; all had normal Apgar scores at 1 minute and at 5 minutes after birth, (9 and 10 or 10 and 10). As originally planned in the first phase of what became the longitudinal study (n=131) each mother brought her infant to be observed and to receive developmental tests at three ages after the neonatal period, that is, at 6, 26, and 52 weeks and annually at ages 4 through 7 years. In the second phase of the study, 23 more children were also observed at ages 2 and/or 3; each mother agreed to be interviewed on the agreed upon dates, about the infant's or child's behavior and progress since the previous meeting. Then, the subjects were to be interviewed at age 18. From time to time, at the mother's request, the date of a meeting was changed, as noted.

Subject 1: Lori: Voyeurism

BO: 2/2
SES: Upper

Lori was socially over-stimulated from early infancy by her M's encouragement to watch and respond to M's facial expressions and voice. She developed a need to look at family members, dressed or undressed, and to be looked at.

Confinement visit with M, Infant age 3 days

M related eagerly to E, volunteering much information about her history, family, and opinions, along with firm ideas about child rearing with an emphasis on permissiveness. As to her probable strength as a mother, she was quick to cite patience and understanding; her probable weakness was to be over-protective and to feel too guilty if her own behaviors were not ideal.

Lori's appearance at birth was attractive, her skin color and the vigor of her movements were excellent, as was her response to feeding. She was alert, visual fixation was brief, auditory and tactile reactions were present most of the time; tension was normal. The degree of her spontaneous movements was also very good.

Age 6 weeks

Lori was small, pale, and a bit tense. Her alertness was pronounced, her visual responses superior, and she showed an unusual variety of facial expressions. Lying prone she could not support her head well; M explained that she rarely left Lori in that position because she didn't like it. M never left her alone; she would carry Lori along with her from room to room. She wanted E to know that the observed fussing was not because of neglect, and spoke continuously to Lori until the baby fell asleep.

Sleep was always induced with a pacifier; if Lori lost it, she "screamed" until it was retrieved. Sometimes she fretted in the evenings and did not sleep through the night, so M held, cuddled, and talked to her until sleep returned. During the day M played with her a great deal, talking and singing to her, and encouraging her to pay attention to people and to playthings. Her handling of the baby was very competent but too quick, too watchful, and too solicitous.

Age 12 weeks[18]

On arrival, M busied herself with smoking, having coffee, making telephone calls, and telling about family problems. It required repeated efforts to bring her attention to the baby. When first given a bottle Lori cried, "chewed" the nipple and spat it out, so M gave her a pacifier, something she often did; she intended to use the pacifier as long as Lori wanted it. She described the baby as "wildly enthusiastic" about people, and was sure that Lori smiled reciprocally, trying to imitate M's mouth movements, but if no one paid attention to her she became irritable. She often wanted to be picked up, and when dissatisfied with the pacifier she comforted herself by sucking her fingers. M was quick to say that in fact Lori got so much comforting from other people that she really didn't have to comfort herself, adding that Lori was "lovely, sweet, gay, and fun-loving."

Age 6 months

Lori was small and physically immature, but could execute many body movements in the prone and supine positions smoothly. Her test behavior was uneven; in the supine she responded to test objects immediately, but at the test table her responses were delayed by her long gazing at and then mouthing of the objects. She was not attentive to E's demonstrations; often she looked away to smile at M or E. This social activity absorbed her, and while she gazed about she expressed many breath sounds, trills, and gurgles. As time went on, her vocal activity became louder, clearer, and stronger.

Lori did not like to sit in the infant seat after eating, M said, and was hard to hold on M's lap because she squirmed so much

---

[18]Before each scheduled visit, M asked for a change in the date of her visit with Lori.

(on observation, she sat for forty minutes in the infant seat with no complaint). She rarely cried, but sometimes if she had to wait too long she burst into tears, so M gave her the pacifier; it always helped her fall asleep. Maybe she could do without it, M said, but M didn't want to impose any needless frustration on her. Everyone in the family loved to play with her and she responded by waving her arms and kicking, or banging her legs "violently." The activity she most adored, M said, was to be put on the floor so she could roll from one side of the room to the other.

M said Lori ate well but tended to throw up about once a week when she ate too much. She did not want to hold her bottle or drink from a cup, so M did not press her to do either. Again M reported that everyone in the family played with Lori, and that there was much hugging, kissing, and playing games, all of which aroused her "giggling." Her favorite activity was crawling, which E observed to be more like a belly-flop, as she propelled herself rapidly by getting up on her knees and falling forward on her abdomen. Sometimes in good moods she rocked herself—but "really she was always in a good mood except when hungry"—then she got annoyed and banged things. M's unceasing pressure to relieve Lori from any sort of distress was matched by her exceeding leniency, and inclination to engage the baby in exciting social play.

Age 1 year

Lori's visual responses to test objects were quick but brief. E had to work rapidly to keep her attention; hiding objects behind the glass made her very impatient. She readily shook the bell and placed the pellet in the bottle, but put no other test object to use, and used only one hand at a time, as if her energy was restricted except in her stereotypical mouthing of all objects. Her frustration tolerance was low. She did not watch E's demonstrations. M said that when Lori became hungry she screamed until food was given to her. Sometimes M gave her a toy to help her wait, but then had to keep on offering new ones or had to hold Lori until the food was ready; if not, she said, Lori became "hysterical." She also screamed when her diaper was changed, pulled away, and made the procedure very difficult. (E observed the baby to be entirely relaxed during a diaper change.) M's feeding was quick and competent, but she was overactive and over-talkative until Lori made definite her refusal of more food. She had become more active, liked pulling things from cabinets, but loved best of all to play physical games with M and F. "She goes into ecstasies about it." Her eagerness to be picked up at all times was immature. Her expressive behavior was most conspicuous in her making faces (as M did), vocalizing, laughing loudly, drawing breath inward, turning her head backward and looking upward. All of this unusual excitement and intense vocal communication between her and M contrasted strongly to her silence when apart from M. Her irritability was unusually quick to appear, her demands were peremptory, and if immediate gratification was not forthcoming or if she was told not to touch something, she seemed ready to hit M in anger. She appeared to have no capacity to comfort herself and needed continuous reassurance, which M kept providing.

M said Lori was enormously curious about new rooms, new bags, etc., and always wanted new territory to cover—"She's not a watcher." (As E observed, Lori neither rummaged in M's handbag nor explored the room at all; she only looked under M's chair or towards the door.) She was not yet standing nor could she pull herself to sit, and her method of crawling was immature and limited in range. She stayed very close to M and made no attempt to walk even when both her hands were held. Her capacity to play alone appeared to be limited, the use of her body was immature, and her demand for comforting excessive.

Age 3 years

Lori was tall and slender, very animated, and readily showed a variety of facial expressions, but her speech was babyish and whiney. Instead of going to the test table she crawled onto M's lap, making many facial gestures, especially with her tongue, as if she were chewing something, and making noises with her mouth. Once persuaded to sit at the table, she continued to whine and became so resistive that all of the tests had to be administered gingerly. She carried out most of them, then wanted M to do them as well; if M did not comply, Lori lost interest in them. Most of the time she was standing or kneeling, active and restless. During the break she ate cookies, refused milk, asking for apple or orange juice instead. She was unusually active, rolling from one side of the bed to the other, kicking, lunging forward to reach objects, then suddenly ceasing activity and gazing intently at something in the room or at E. Her vocalizations consisted of loud shrieks, screams and sobbing. M tried to comfort her by more feeding, then finally gave up.

M said Lori had walked and begun to speak at sixteen months, had always been very well coordinated, loved dancing, singing, and doing puzzles and that her favorite activity was running. She accepted few foods, mainly sweets, drinks, and hot dogs, but no milk. If M required her to taste any other foods she spat them out. Her sleep was light. She awoke at any sound, sometimes going back to sleep easily, at other times crying "hysterically," calling M to get her a drink or some food. This kind of "random shrieking," began when she was a little past two. Sometimes during the night she walked to M's bed. M usually took her back to her own bed, though sometimes she stayed in M's bed until the morning, or she stayed awake for hours, walking back and forth between her own bed and M's. She had numerous ruses to get M out of bed. Because of this kind of unruly behavior several maids had left; one had "made [Lori] cry so much that she vomited." About the vomiting M added excusingly that Lori had "a small, funny tendency not to chew things."

The child began to give up her pacifier three or four months earlier but often asked for it back. She had always been "very verbal and always used the first person singular," and could carry on conversations excellently with all kinds of people. She loved to dress up in M's clothing, acting the part of mother, baby, queen, or dancer. She could play by herself and needed no amusement, M said with praise, but when asked not to do something she wished to do, she screamed, "Don't tell me!" scowled, became angry enough to kick, and in such a state once spat at a maid. "But she didn't really have temper tantrums," M said, adding that she was a wonderful child, very affectionate verbally and physically. She could get extremely angry and stubborn about what she wanted to do, and if she got angry at any interference with her wishes, she might throw up.

M was hard-pressed to think of any habits that Lori had, yet told of her habitually teasing her sister Jane by standing in front of the television so that Jane could not watch it. She also pinched, nudged, and picked and poked at her sister. M said spanking was a token, and let the child know what was desired, and believed that Lori could control herself only if removed from temptation, and was easy to deal with, though unhappy when told she could not do something that her sister was doing. Sometimes in new situations she was scared and hid her face in M's skirt, which M said "was just a game." At the end of the testing, M seemed bored, or perhaps overwhelmed by Lori's demands. There was an undertone of didacticism in her statements about child rearing and she blamed her mistakes on her acceptance of bad advice from teachers and doctors.

F thought that at first school might put a strain on Lori, but a structured situation would be good for her. He thought she was a very easy child to be with, although in recent months at bedtime she ran around for about half an hour before getting into bed, and always asked for some sort of comfort until his patience wore out. Especially at 3:30 AM, he said, it was hard for him not to be annoyed. Each morning she would call her parents to bring her into their bed. He found these interruptions quite disturbing, and went on to say that he enjoyed traveling because it allowed him to get a full night's sleep. Her sister Jane loved books and complicated toys, but Lori was "strictly for pleasure, with a very short attention span." She enjoyed strenuous activities—running, hiding, and wrestling; she was "a tough kid," not at all introspective. She asked questions just for the sake of asking, paying little attention to the answers, was very stubborn, and wouldn't do something she didn't want to unless he spoke to her very sharply. "She knew her own mind," and he liked this about her; on the other hand, she could be distracted too quickly. Sometimes she cried hard to the point of vomiting.

When it was time to leave the playground, she screamed, so that he had to pick her up firmly, pin her arms to her sides, and talk to her about other things. He had also locked the door of her room to prevent her coming into her parents' bed in the morning—then she cried and vomited. He did not see anything inadequate about her frustration tolerance, he rather took it as a sign of her tough-mindedness. He had been firmly opposed to any use of force, yet as Lori grew older his patience was wearing thin, so that now he felt "it was good for parents to spank once or twice—it was a necessary expression of a pent-up parent." She did not cry easily, and he took this as another sign of her strength. He could not think of anything she was afraid of. She never stopped talking although she had little to say—"it was just a kind of constant rambling." He thought of her as fearless, happy, and never embarrassed. Embarrassment was "not her thing," because "she was not introspective—emotions would not get in her way."

Observation in school: Age 3 years, 7 months

Lori hid behind M, wanting her not to leave the foyer. After more time M said, "OK, lamb chop, give me a hug and a kiss, I have to go." Lori kissed M profusely on her coat and all over her leg, until finally M disentangled herself. Then Lori wandered about the room, undirected, uneasy, and using her Slinky to help her connect with a series of classmates. She spent long periods standing alone, chewing on her lip, or picking her nose nervously; finally asked to paint, she chose colors haphazardly, concentrating on filling up all the spaces on the paper, then walked away with no thought of looking at what she had produced. She went to another child who was using clay, and rolled longer and longer "snakes," calling them bracelets, or necklaces. Her mood was guarded, worried, and sullen. Often she chewed on her lips or tongue, kept a hand in her mouth, rubbed her eyes, poked at her face, made funny faces, or picked her nose, all conveying a state of continuous anxiety. Her social judgment was poor. When another girl tried to touch her in a friendly way, Lori at once showed hurt feelings. At another time, the same girl wanted to take her hand and dance around with her; Lori was annoyed. Nor did she join in group play. It seemed that once having declined offers to play with others, she had to save face by not accepting any friendly overtures. During juice time, she drank just a little, became restless, stood up, sat down, and rubbed her eyes. Occasionally she became involved with some material, but her activity was never infused with much purpose.

Age 4 years, 5 months

Lori carried out test tasks smoothly, but she was restless, impulsive, and distractible. When aware of an error she quickly covered it with her hand, and working very slowly said defiantly, "I can do it as slow as I can." Her facial expression was serious and a little harsh, and as soon as items became somewhat difficult, she "dropped out." Her scores on the WRAT were minimal. For much of the time she cared little about her performance. She talked a great deal, often asking E questions that had no meaning for her. She handled materials roughly, fidgeted, and refused tasks. She was extremely verbal, silly, or restless; she kicked her feet, got up and down, or slapped the test table. On the Stanford-Binet, her estimated IQ was 137, possibly heightened by her verbal ability.

M maintained a rigid, controlled, bored look throughout the time Lori was being tested, but when E told her Lori had done well, she became friendly, and said she had had no worry about Lori's abilities. She said Lori's diet was self-restricted to mainly sweets, pastas, and many kinds of drinks. Every few months she asked M to feed her, then resisted M's help. When M ate something new, Lori would try it. Sometimes she called for M during the night, or if her parents were out in the evening, on their return they found her in their bed. She had become extremely modest about being seen naked or on the toilet, but had shown increased interest and excitement about anything having to do with sexuality or toileting. She tried to enter the bathroom whenever M or grandmother were there, and when M was bathing she stared at M's body intently until asked to leave. At home she invariably stayed near M, looked at a book or played with M's shoes or jewelry. She became rebellious when restricted, then half-heartedly tried to slap M. In these instances M tried not to be stern lest Lori get angrier, yet sometimes M lost patience and gave her a "whack" on her "buttocks." She had had a few tantrums recently. Once, her parents allowed her to "scream it out," then intervened after fifteen minutes, telling her to stop it, which she did at once. She no longer bathed with Jane because they became too raucous as they played "sexual games." She had begun to make an issue of what clothing to wear, and cried if not permitted to wear something of her choice. She was extraordinarily jealous of M. When M dressed to go out, Lori would say, "You look pretty," and sob about it. M seemed to derive excitement from finding the child "in the midst of an Oedipal conflict." The chief reason for discipline was her teasing of her sister. One "whack" on her behind was effective, though it might make her angrier. Still, M thought Lori had pretty good self-control because when she slapped at M in anger, she did so lightly, so the slap was "only symbolic."

F reported that Lori's appetite was very good, and that though she still vomited when upset, this behavior had become much more infrequent in the last year. Lori insisted on making her own decisions about her clothing, and promised to vomit if not allowed to have her way; once she threatened to vomit over F's leather boots. He considered her frustration tolerance "barely adequate;" yet discipline was needed most when she dawdled at bedtime or teased her sister too much. Then he might speak sharply to her, or give her a light "whack" on her behind. He said her self-control had improved, then told that a succession of maids had left because of her misbehaviors. M was seen naked; F was not, and Lori was so curious about him that when he was dressing or in his shorts she tried to stand in front of him to see what she could, became angry when stopped, and screamed. F had a suave and charming manner but was not at ease. By preference he sat in a swivel chair and moved about in it restlessly. Some of his observations were given with a kind of amused condescension. He deplored M's over-involvement with the children, as well as her indolence and her unwillingness to leave the children and enjoy trips with him alone.

Age 5 years, 6 months

Lori's countenance was not at all cheerful. She sat with her legs spread far apart, and there was something slow and heavy about her movements. Her voice was exceptionally loud and raucous, and when excited she shrieked. She enunciated every word slowly and with such extraordinary precision that it seemed affected. On arrival she was quite reserved and would not speak to E so that at first M found it necessary to answer E's questions for her. During one of the Performance items, she mischievously peeked while E was setting up materials for the next subtest. Soon she began to clown, contorted her face wildly, made silly noises, hummed or sang nonsense songs, huffed and puffed as if exerting herself terribly, and reacted to each test item presented to her with a loud outburst. She shrieked, "Oh!" or "Ah!" with eyes widened and a huge intake of breath. Or she exclaimed in loud measured tones, affecting a French accent, for example, "Zis is a hardie!" "Zis is fun!" During most of the subtests her resistance was pronounced—she sulked, complained of fatigue, or flatly dismissed items by saying, "I cannot do it, I cannot do it." During Verbal tests she squirmed, rocked, bounced up and down in her chair, tilted it against the wall, stood beside it, fell out of it, stretched her limbs, and wandered about. She also shook her legs, knocked her knees together, tugged at her clothing, chewed on and sucked her fingers, chewed on test materials, clutched her genitals, and continuously engaged in tongue and mouth movements. Rarely did she admit that she didn't know how to answer a question, and often reverted to saying that something was "very hard," without any sign of frustration, seeming to imply that she should not be expected to complete any test item as difficult as the one she confronted. She executed most of them without any apparent motivation to succeed, yawned frequently, rested her head on the test table, complained about being tired, and often. stopped drawing to sing silly songs. She attended well to tasks she found pleasant, otherwise she was quick to withdraw. She had a tendency to smile coyly, and at other times to contort her mouth in ugly scowls. She could speak in a precise and measured manner, but when anxious she engaged in an extraordinary amount of restless and autoerotic behavior. She would shout rather than speak in modulated tones. She hurled objects around aggressively, and was occasionally obstreperous and demanding. E was struck by her decided lack of femininity.

M's appearance was dramatic. Her bleached hair was long and tousled, she wore much eye makeup, and tight-fitting, navy bell-bottomed trousers. She had greeted E enthusiastically upon arrival, and reacted effusively when offered coffee. Her friendliness toward E was extreme. Her behavior toward Lori was overly positive—she smiled at her, called her pet names, and several times interrupted her activity to embrace her. She wrung her hands nervously and appeared hard pressed to think of things to say to Lori. Sometimes her comments were far-fetched, for example, she blurted out to the child, "Look at that teddy! It has the greatest looking face," and at another time, mused with no apparent cause, "I'm trying to think of a toy you played with a lot when you were little."

In the mornings Lori woke her sister against her parents' wishes. She had a great deal of sexual curiosity, liked to look at her sister's genitals, and once she put her hand on M's genitals. M told her not to do that, because that part of the body was very private. She was confused about the vagina and the vulva, which M had tried to explain. She now didn't care if she was seen naked. M was aware that Lori played some voyeuristic games with Jane, and that she was much interested in seeing a visiting little boy undress while he was changing into his bathing suit. At school boys and girls used the same bathroom, so Lori often laughed about penises. Questions about sexual differences were directed to M, who answered them factually. Lori laughed convulsively in response to M's answers. She was still greatly interested in seeing her parents nude, and F found it a burden always to be concerned with his nudity, asking rhetorically what he should do.

She often teased her sister and said, "I hate Jane," although she "worshipped" her in a way, mainly out of jealousy. There was some physical conflict between the two and M at times had to step in to protect both of them. Lori was unruly if not allowed to have a sweet before dinner or to stay up late. She would throw things, stamp her feet, or exclaim "Rats!" or "Damn it!" or "I'm mad at everybody!" Discipline was needed mainly for wild play, then M gave her a "whack" on her behind, sent her to her room, or deprived her of something that she wanted. M had disliked hitting, but now found it "Easy, fast, painless, and effective." Lori resented her parents' going out to parties without her. M again emphasized that Lori was very quick and bright, had a very developed sense of humor, and was "Very, very dear, and cute," adding that she was "winning, loving, affectionate, and intensely proud of her family. I think she's great."

F thought last year was a difficult one for Lori, perhaps because, according to M, the T was unresponsive and rigid. When Lori did not want to go to school, her parents did not force her. When the decision was left to her, she usually went. F said that she already had social assets, was a "well integrated" child, and was extremely competitive. She objected when her parents went out for the evening or for the weekend, and spoke about being in a "down" mood. When criticized, she said she was mad, yelled, cried, and threw things. She was critical of children who offended her in any way and was often disobedient and rebellious if she did not get her own way. Their method of discipline depended on the nature of her offense, and on the parent's temper. At times F, too, had resorted to spanking. He thought she had a strict conscience, but was unsure. He knew she was too aggressive with housekeepers, admitted wrongdoing unwillingly, and yelled out, "I'm sorry," without any show of remorse. F was sophisticated but low-keyed and distant. When thanked for his time, he replied with a mixture of good manners and sincerity that he liked these interviews because they made him think. He conveyed the impression of being a removed spectator of his family. He said little spontaneously.

Observation in school: Age 5 years, 1 month

Lori had been particularly "cranky" this morning and had not wanted to go to school. Once there, her mood vacillated between irritability and smiles. She was capricious in relating to her classmates, at times friendly and helpful, then condescending and rude. She clung to objects she had brought from home, demanded much attention from the teacher, voiced a number of both real and apparently imaginary complaints, and sometimes seemed lost. She managed a woodworking project with imagination, skill and determination, having waited for a turn at the tool bench for two days. After such concentrated effort her activity declined; then she wandered about the room, making random social contacts, few of them pleasant, as she interfered with other children's work. During a period of free play, she seemed at a loss when nothing to do presented itself to her immediately, then began activities in imitation of other children. She found it hard to sit still, often left her seat to talk with other children or the T, and constantly toyed with her bracelet. She refused to take part in rhythm activities because it made her mouth hurt, and then whined to the teacher, "Oh, I can't jump, I can't do it." She could be the ablest of diplomats or the rudest of companions. A few times she resolved minor conflicts between other children tactfully. When a group of children were at the table drawing, and there was not enough space for the materials some squabbling ensued, whereupon she calmly explained that "everyone could share the crayons," then offered to move to the other end of the table so that everyone could have room. She was subtly controlling, and often engaged in passing physical contacts with people. For example, she brushed very gently against them as she walked past, or absently stroked the arm of a person with whom she was talking. It was as if she craved contact and affection yet almost without fail wore a frown when listening to others speak, as if she had some difficulty in hearing. When sometimes praised for her work, she remarked, "I draw like my sister." She drew a windmill and presented it as her own work; it turned out to be a copy of something her sister had done at home the day before. She appeared loath to admit any deficiency and her air of self-possession seemed not quite real. T said that she used to be altogether dependent on an adult's help to get through a task, still often complained that she had nothing to do, or at an advantageous moment said she had some physical ailment. On this day, for example, when she became tired of the group activities, she complained almost incessantly that her mouth hurt.

Age 6 years, 2 months

Lori's speech was distinct. She spoke a lot using a large vocabulary with frequent references to foreign places and events. During the Verbal section of the WISC tests she was quite restless; during the Performance section she was calm to the point of weariness, complaining that her legs were strained from sitting so long. When E made no reply she added that her stomach and head also hurt. E told her she could walk around the room for a bit. She made no further complaints and sat down to finish her testing, but occasionally rested her face on her elbows or laid her head on the table. After a time she insisted that the items were "Very, very hard." She did make an effort to succeed, but carried on a continuous monologue, a typical part of which was "...This is a car ...I don't know this ...This is very hard ...Oh boy, I don't think this is right ...I know that goes there, but what else? ...There has to be some way... I don't know, it's hard to do this ...I don't know this but I'm trying..." At other times she made clicking noises with her tongue or hummed little happy tunes as she worked, though her movements were lethargic. She repeatedly made the same errors on the Object Assembly even though it was obvious to her that she was not doing the right thing. If she had not shown such superior ability in the Verbal realm, or if her motor coordination had been impaired, her behavior on the Performance section would not have been so strange.

During the CAT she was extremely restless, moved about constantly in her chair, scratched her hair, rubbed her eye, clutched her genitals, and finally picked up her skirt and chewed on the hem. She tended to be impulsive and to have a predominant need to stand up. When asked what she liked most of all, she said it was the pie that her housekeeper made, then went on in grand elaboration of the types of pies. After the Picture Completion, she became slow, leaned her head against the table, and seemed to have suddenly lost confidence (she apparently knew that she was not achieving well). When M came to the observation room to get her, she was stretched out on the floor on her stomach and did not move because she had become engrossed in drawing Queen Elizabeth. She said goodbye five times before reaching the door. M was cordial in response to E, and effusive in response to Lori, saying things such as, "Oh you got that. You're absolutely right. You're absolutely right." At the end of the M-C play, the child looked around and said, "Now what? I'm finished." M replied "You're finished? Looks like a nice schoolhouse!" Throughout their time together, they smiled and laughed. M not only complimented Lori, she took hold of her hand, squeezed it and gave it a kiss. Occasionally she allowed Lori to stay home because of their shared dislike of the T. The child could be self sufficient about preparing for bed, yet often said she was tired so as to have M's help, and still dawdled. Sometimes she had a "fun bath" with Jane, and continued to enter the bathroom to stare at M's body, though M strongly discouraged it. She was extremely conscious of clothing, jewelry, and hair, worried that she was "fat, not pretty and didn't have nice clothing," and was critical of M for being prettier than she and wearing nicer clothing. M became angry because of Lori's ungenerous attitude, so now she rarely interfered with the child's choice of daily clothing, even when she selected ridiculous combinations. She still described Lori as "irresistibly lovable."

She said Lori was a big tease; she mimicked and engaged in self-parody, for example, making believe she was a baby. M found this endearing. She made funny faces, assumed accents, loved jokes and roughhousing. Her manners were good, but she was easily insulted, as when an aunt called her "a little actress." When alone she might draw or look at books, was very proud of things she made, and could accept correction if given gently. At first M said Lori had not expressed any ambition for grown-up work, then recalled that she had spoken of becoming a singer or an actress. (M was now taking acting lessons and believed this had stirred Lori's interest.) She described Lori as characteristically "excited and joyful or active and busy, rarely quiet and thoughtful." She was a chatterbox, and was miffed if M told her to stop talking for a while. In response she at times said, "You are not a good mother" or went to her room and cried. She also cried when punished, and stayed mad for up to half an hour. She could admit wrongdoing, but not readily. She now bit her nails and then tried to hide them from M, who had heard her criticize herself about her appearance but not about her behavior.

M presented herself as open, candid and emotionally free, but always seemed to be role-playing with a studied spontaneity. At first she had seemed interested and involved, then became progressively more self-contained until she seemed impatient and eager to finish. Typically, she had tried to put a time limit on her interviews, making E aware of her pressing schedule. Her reports were economical, with intermittent bursts of extravagant praise. M declared herself to be "utterly delighted" with Lori as she was "universally loved…everyone's child…and a child for everyone."

F said Lori liked school but was often reluctant to go, complaining that her teacher was not fair to her and that she didn't like lunch at school, he said, because she had to eat more than she wanted. When he had been separated from Lori regularly during the winter to go skiing she missed him a lot, and although he telephoned daily, she sometimes refused to talk to him. Occasionally she had dinner with her parents, and wanted to be excused from the table as soon as she finished eating, or to leave her chair to sit on F's lap, which he allowed. At bedtime she always wanted someone to sit on her bed, and needed a nightlight in her room as well as in the hallway. She got up several times to go to the bathroom, to get a drink, or to get something else. When she complained that she couldn't sleep, one of her parents or a housekeeper sat with her for a while, or she was allowed to stay out of bed and talk briefly with them. F had recently become aware that Lori was very competitive with M, complaining that M was prettier than she, and had nicer clothing. She did not like M and F to be alone together. When alone at home, she might bang on the piano, or pull out all her toys or dress up in costumes. If she wanted to do something she usually rushed ahead rather than planning her actions, he said. Her mood was usually excited and joyful, seldom quiet and thoughtful, angry when she didn't get her way, and self-critical mostly in reference to not being pretty, or too fat, or "not doing anything right." F was courteous, passive, acquiescent, but impersonal and remote.

Observation in School: Age 6 years, 11 months

During group discussions, Lori concentrated well enough to know what was going on, but chatted with her classmate whenever possible, was disinterested in listening to the T and often looked annoyed. She ignored O altogether, occasionally glancing in her direction before looking away disinterestedly. Once, as she left the group to get a tissue, she brushed by O's chair and scowled, as if to say, "Who on earth are you and what are you doing here?" She usually looked serious, often frowned, and stormed around the room as if challenging something or someone to bring her pleasure. It appeared to be a habit for her to sit with a grumpy expression on her face while she observed other children or thought about what to do next. She seemed to show affection for friends by holding hands during group discussions or the playground, and once by stroking her friend's face. During conversations she smiled and laughed a great deal; a moment later seemed dissatisfied, frowned and looked solemn.

Observation in school: Age 7 years, 1 month

Lori's dress was casual, almost careless. She wore a very skimpy pair of shorts, and sneakers with holes in them. There was to be a school outing on this day, so that it might appear that she was dressed appropriately, but the weather was windy, and showed indications of rain. She was less than fully attentive to fine motor tasks, lacking motivation and commitment.

M had been notified about the date for Lori's observation but on that day Lori did not arrive at school. When called to be told that a project staff member was waiting for her in the classroom, M was rude and abusive in her language, cursed, used profanities, and was totally taken aback to hear that this was indeed the day for the psychologist to see Lori. She did not know whether Lori had already left for school. After she gathered herself together, she phoned our office to cancel the visit, only to be told that Lori was already in school. Lori meanwhile said she did not wish to be tested, as M had told her she need not. After the school director cajoled her into proceeding with the test, she complained that she had gone through this procedure too many times, gave minimal attention to the first questions, seemed to be working only toward the goal of having this unpleasant experience done with. During the test she got up and walked away from the table. On the WRAT her reading score could be converted to a grade of 2.1, her spelling to a grade of 1.8, scores that were minimal in terms of her real ability.

M refused to come for her last interview, she was the only M who did this out of a full sample of 131. E surmised that this was either because she was bored with the testing situation, because she was again expressing her negative attitude toward authority, and/or because she had become unhappily aware that Lori's behavior was not so ideal as she had presumed.

Tests, Age 18 years

Lori was youthful in appearance, but had a sophisticated quality about her presentation of herself. She was lively and described many interests, but was somewhat scattered in her conversation. She expressed various ambitions, for example about college acceptances, and made use of sarcastic humor, as when she jokingly asked about one of the tests, "Is this some kind of Freudian thing?" She was discouraged by any task she found difficult, and took a somewhat aggressive posture, stating with bravura, "Sometimes I just can't get something." At times she approached material in a systematic, organized way, at other times was impressionistic and vague. A degree of emotional lability characterized her associations, but they were never bizarre. Sometimes this manner seemed cultivated, as if it gave her pleasure to try to shock the listener, or be "artsy" in style.

On the WAIS-R she achieved a full scale IQ of only 107. There was little variability that would suggest much higher potential not being utilized, but there were many indications of interference with effectiveness, from a mixture of obsessive doubting to vague, impressionistic guessing. Her learning to date was probably adequate if not impressive. It appeared that when her capacities, interests, and emotional life came together, she could be something of a powerhouse, but inconsistently. In formal contexts she was led to a degree of "silliness," of personalized associations, and, when uncertain, she became distracted. Though she managed to complete most of the tasks, she had consistent difficulties in reasoning. In the less structured projective tests, she was more comfortable because associating and offering her impressions were more familiar to her. It was possible to see here the degree of disorganization and regression of which she was capable. Her responses to the projective tests indicated a lack of self-protective organization; she was very responsive to emotional stimulation, fantasy, and personal interaction. This was a strong positive quality, in that she was imaginative, lively, responsive, and creative, but at times she appeared vulnerable to impulse and affect. She could draw on intellectual defenses (for example, seeing the TAT cards as movie stills) to maintain needed distance, but this attitude served for rationalizations and did not help protect her from being swamped by rather primitive defenses. While she showed a capacity for mundane experiences, there was a much darker, more complicated, less well-controlled side in her fantasy life. Sudden eruptions of violent competitiveness with her sibling appeared, as did occasional regressions in form and content regarding sadistic impulses. Her hysterical personality style led her to react with some shock to the color in card 2 on the Rorschach. She could pleasantly say, "Bleeding buffalo," and later comfortably rationalize this response in terms of a painting her F had done. There appeared to be considerable conflict in her strong identification with M; it was consistently negative, yet mixed with yearnings for closeness and an idealized, little-girl conception of mother-daughter interactions. Men were seen as appealing and frightening; she alternately idealized and depreciated them.

Diagnostic statement

Hysterical personality with current exacerbated conflict and capacity for regression, quite possibly developmentally-determined.

Lori appeared to be dealing with a range of adolescent turmoil, and psychosexual as well as identity issues, coming to them with a mixed array of defensive abilities, and to have a generally hysterically organized personality structure with at least average intellectual capacity and probably real creative potential. Without more knowledge of her real life it was difficult to differentiate the sensitivity and creativity of an artistic adolescent struggling with her emotions, from the disorganization of a more borderline personality organization. Certainly she was in a state of emotional lability and great flux. She was aroused by impulses and affects, and could easily regress to more primitive methods of expression, at least in fantasy. There was considerable conflict about sexual and other identificatory processes, and much capacity for anger, yet this might all be part of the working-through of age and phase-appropriate tasks in the context of a vibrant, sensitive, but basically strong personality.

Interview, Age 18 years

Lori was a short, overweight young woman, somewhat unkempt in a loose, large overshirt, tight jeans, high boots with heels, and very ostentatious large earrings. Her complexion was blemished, her voice deep and grating.

She described the private school she had previously attended and could not praise it highly enough. In tenth grade, however, she had feared that her marks were going down and that she would not get into a good enough college, so she transferred in her junior year to a different school where "half of the students were sons or daughters of diplomats and ambassadors from all over the world." Lori felt the new school to be a strange place because of the formal dress of the teachers, and because "so many people didn't know what was going on, and nothing happened." She was immediately at the top of the class, which she considered "pretty silly." There was no self-criticism for her poor work at the previous school, only criticism of the other students for being so competitive. The new school was also competitive, but "in a sterile way."

Reading had been limited because of schoolwork, but when she was bored she might pick up something to read. She never had any chores at home because when she was younger "the family was very wealthy; they had had three houses with maids, a butler and a chauffeur. Now they had just a housekeeper." When a few years ago M asked her to take something out of the dishwasher she didn't know what that meant. "I never had to make a bed." At sixteen, she had worked in a clothing store for a year as "sales manager," then did clerical work for a publisher, but decided not to go back because the office was too far for her to go (about six miles away). During one summer she went abroad for twelve weeks. In the coming summer, she expected to stay in Los Angeles for a month. She had applied to six colleges. Her SATs were 400 in Math, "the best mark in school," and 600 in English. She had thought of majoring in journalism because she enjoyed psychology and sociology, liked to write, and was also interested in law. With her friends she played tennis, went to Chinatown, looked at television, and went to "famous bars."

She had begun to menstruate at age nine and thought she had gotten her knowledge about sex from friends at school, reading popular novels, and maybe from M. Lori's answer about sexual education was that she could go to either parent, or they could go to her. She answered this question quickly, almost with a wave of her hand, as though it need not even be talked about. When she was a child her parents had separated for a short time. Again, for the past nine months F had not been living at home, but Lori thought they would soon get back together. There was "no fighting," and "no talk of divorce"; each parent "just needed breathing space." Her whole family was eccentric. One Christmas morning, for example, F suddenly called and said, "Pack your bags, we're going to London in an hour."

She described M as "arrogant, making fun of people, but also warm, lovable, and very smart." Lori herself was too quick to get angry and didn't have much patience—if she was ready to go somewhere, she couldn't wait for anybody else. It made her feel crazy if she had to wait. She was much irritated by noises, crowds, and annoying people. She knew she was arrogant, "in a funny way," but added "I can't deal with things I don't want to deal with....What irritates me also amuses me." She had "lots and lots and lots of friends." She liked to have structure and work, "but not silly work," as in the present school. She could be made happy even just walking down the street, had tantrums, yelled and screamed, but never hit. She had a big mouth, not for foul language, but could speak cuttingly. She liked her sense of humor and the fact that she was very forgiving and easy to be with, but not her shyness on first meeting people. About herself she disliked only her weight and her impatience. "And sometimes I judge people from the outside...If people aren't wearing the right clothing or don't look right, or don't like the right music." She had never thought about her conscience. "It's just there. Really there's no such thing. It's just you. It's not something to balance you out. If I'm thinking about my conscience, it's unconscious. It's just really me." She had smoked marijuana at thirteen or fourteen, tried cocaine but didn't enjoy it, smoked cigarettes for five years and stopped about seven weeks ago when she realized it was just out of habit. She liked to drink but didn't get sick.

She definitely wanted children, didn't know how many, but surely not just one. "You always have to have someone around. They should go to a good school, and should have a top education." There was nothing about her childhood that she would want to change. She went on to express one platitude after another: "You should know that not everybody is out to get you...You should do the best you can and not live in the past...War is unhealthy for children." In ethics class at school she had to talk a great deal about capital punishment. She hoped to be someone who would change the world, "maybe a reporter for something like Watergate." She could not think of any famous person she admired, then said that she admired all intelligent people who knew what they wanted, and had the drive, determination, and patience to get it.

Clinical Impression

After my above dictation, I realized how disturbed Lori was. She was overly dedicated to the interview, yet her reports were suffused with denials and many all-or-nothing statements, such as "I'm irritated by nothing and I regret nothing." Often there was evidence of a disturbance in her thinking, almost enough to suggest that she might have a borderline personality disorder. A show of overconfidence was apparent most of the time. Her statement that she left one of the finest high schools after two years because it was so hard and because she had to get into a good college could not be the whole story. For a girl who aspired to be either a journalist or a writer, there was something odd in her leaving a school where the competition was high just in order to get A's, and M, who was upwardly mobile, would not have liked her to leave a fine school for a small and poor one. Probably it was after many of her friends and her sister had graduated from high school, when she was supposed to go into the 11th grade, that she did not wish to stay. Her need to denigrate people and situations gave the impression that she was profoundly fearful of praising anyone other than her family and close friends.

Her intelligence appeared to be good, but she was overexcited, exhibitionistic, hysterical, highly narcissistic, and appeared to be making an effort to hold down anxiety that might intrude into almost every aspect of her life, with the possible exception of fun with friends. One may judge that this young woman had an extreme need to show her knowledge of the world around her (a mark of her voyeurism) and to declare her emotional security, the value of her intentions, the excellence of her relationships, and her conviction of one day attaining excellence in whatever she chose to do. The elation she showed about herself strikingly resembled her M's name-dropping and convictions of uniqueness.

Figure 1: Age 4; Agirl.

Figure 2: Age 5; A girl.

Figure 3: Age 5; Her family.

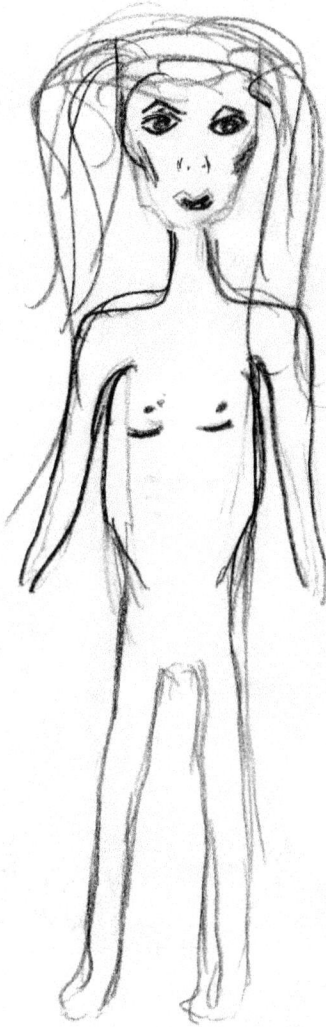

Figure 4: Age 18; Person of the same sex.

Figure 5: Age 18; Person of the opposite sex.

Analysis of Lori's Drawings: Voyeurism

Lori's figure drawings at age 5 are in contrast to her drawing of a figure at 4 years old. Her earliest drawing is large and uninhibited, with large eyes and a chaotically drawn mouth. This is in line with her early presentation of a talkative, restless, and impulsive little girl. A year later, her figure drawings are strikingly smaller, with an effort at tight control and a feeling of the compressed, slowed movement and barely-clenched emotion that she demonstrated at this age. Her drawing of a girl is odd in its emphasis on an exaggerated neck, and long, phallic-like arm-hand extensions, suggesting her early conflict around withdrawal and attention seeking.

In a family drawing, she and her sister have chaotically drawn faces, with gaping, repetitively circled mouths and no necks. Heavy phallic-like arms are again prominent, perhaps indicating Lori's frenetic, yet clumsy attempts to achieve cognitively and to relate to those closest to her. He mother appears as a phallic, neck-less form, with heavy phallic arms and an overly wide smile. The figure of the mother is dominant, taking up the space with a sort of unspecified embrace, as her mother was so intrusive and disruptive in her early years. A father floats at the top of the page, as Lori's father stayed on the edges of her life.

Her drawings in adolescence are intensely disturbing, appearing as lightly drawn and unfinished anatomical sketches of debilitated, emaciated corpses. A female figure is displayed in a full frontal view, without either clothing or anatomically correct genital or physical detail. In the pelvic region, a few lines hint at pubic hair. The figure's cheekbones and ribs are heavily emphasized, with prominent over-sized heavy-lidded, tired eyes. The neck is elongated and the hands are entirely absent, indicating a strongly attempted distance from impulses. The combination of details suggests a young pre-pubescent girl, uncomfortable, physically preoccupied by insecurity and deficits, yet on display. Lori's lack of self-protectiveness and her regression in response to emotional and relational material are also indicated in this drawing of a naked little girl. A male figure is even more disturbingly displayed, yet unfinished, also demonstrating an ongoing conflict for Lori in her wishes and fears around relationships with male figures, including her distanced father. A facial profile with a prominent nose appears severe yet disconnected. The male body consists of no more than a skinny handless arm, the line of the chest, and an equally skinny impotent appendage suggesting a footless leg. The drawing is described by her as a "profile," but is in fact little more than a male head with the repeated suggestion of what is absent and unknown.

In her adolescent drawings, male and female, both the desire to explore the anatomy and an avoidance of the mature male and female form is evident. These drawings are simultaneously weak and suggestive, in line with her competing desires to see and not be seen. The ungrounded figures also hint at Lori's own shallow sense of self and difficulty placing herself in the world.

Synopsis

Throughout her childhood Lori was overindulged and over praised by M who encouraged the child to watch and mimic her facial expressions, and to be overactive socially. F stayed in the background with no idea about how to help Lori behave appropriately. Her need to look at family members, dressed or undressed, was present in her early years. She tried again and again to watch her mother and grandmother while they were bathing, her father and sister while they changed clothing, as well as the undressing of a visiting boy of her own age. That voyeurism was naturally complemented by her need to be looked at and praised highly. Probably in response to her mother's constant admiration, Lori became excessively proud of everything she knew, did or had. Excessive speech was a mark of her continuous social excitement. In spite of high intelligence, her remarks were often loose or incoherent, and suggested overweening self-satisfaction. I felt continuously aware of her excessive need to elaborate on all her statements effusively.

Subject 2: Edwin: Exhibitionism, Moderate

BO: 2/4
SES: Upper

Edwin's early development was superior, aided by M's gentle and thoughtful care. His exhibitionism, which appeared at the end of his early childhood, stemmed from difficulties between his parents that brought about the lowering of his aspirations.

Confinement visit with M, Infant age 3 days

M had met F at a university party, had disliked him intensely, thought he was too smooth, but married him after three years. She had enjoyed working in several medical research clinics, had no knowledge of infant care, but hoped to recognize any traits in her children that she disapproved of in herself. She wanted them to be "strong, healthy, bright and all the rest of those things," as well as generous and sympathetic toward others. "It sounds very much like a Victorian strong character, doesn't it?" she said, with good humor. M was a pleasant, cheerful, and cooperative subject, though she said very little about her feelings.

Edwin showed unusual freedom to move parts of his body. His visual, auditory, and tactile responses and movements were all excellent. He moved his head easily, was normally active, not at all irritable, and was at all times alert. His color was good, his visual fixation was obtained with some difficulty; all other responses were positive and he had been accepting breastfeeding adequately. M was very pleased with his quietness.

Age 5 weeks, 1 day

Edwin's attention to objects was immediate and prolonged. He fixated on E, followed her as she walked away, and smiled at her when she spoke to him. His body was limp when he was pulled to sitting, with considerable head-lag, but his activity increased when he was dressed or undressed. He was very alert, enjoyed looking around the room a great deal, at E, and at whomever else was present. M said he only fussed when very hungry, and could be comforted by her placing a hot water bottle on his tummy; then he fell asleep. He cried but never screamed. She wished she could have been better prepared for his occasional irritability, felt sure she must be doing something wrong, but as her first baby had behaved similarly, she tried not to worry about it. She handled Edwin and spoke to him gently, rarely stimulated him more than to jiggle his body a little or to speak to him with pleasure. He was alert and responsive, well developed in all areas, an unusually contented baby.

Age 6 months

Edwin had become big and husky. On arrival he stared at E for some fifteen minutes. Although his behavior lacked vitality, once persuaded to look at test objects his reactions were quick and eager, his attention span long. With persuasion, E was able to elicit his attention and a full-faced smile. Both parents and his nurse played with him briefly each morning, then he played by himself for ten to twenty minutes while sitting in his high chair. M said he always showed happy excitement when he had things to play with, especially a cloth book that he liked to crumple up. He often laughed, smiled, and kicked his feet excitedly, had shown particular interest in his toes, which he liked to curl up and hold in his hand, and he liked to look at his hands, holding them together at the mid-line.

Age 1 year

Edwin's gross and fine motor coordination were excellent. He was at his best with items that gave him scope for quick activity. He walked about the room in a very relaxed manner, and appeared to enjoy maneuvering himself into difficult physical places from which he needed to be rescued by M. He enjoyed especially standing with feet apart, putting his head down on the floor, and looking around in an almost flirtatious manner, then turning his face to look at M with a shy smile. She said he could hold his body in this round arch for at least a minute at a time. He seemed to understand immediately what to do with test objects, but failed many times because he was not able to invest energy in completing tasks; mostly he wanted to see new objects and to watch how E handled them. At home he liked best to run around the apartment, look at people, and search in drawers and cupboards. He understood "No" but went right ahead doing what he wanted to do. He liked to play games with anyone at all and to imitate M when she did her morning exercise.

M allowed him to run about, and did not rescue him from physical difficulties unless he became fearful. She spoke of him and other members of the family with little affection though not unkindly, and observed that the children were growing up too fast, so that she felt at a loss when he cried, fearing that he was forcing her to spoil him. He didn't like to be scolded. For example, if he was scolded for standing on his high chair, he put his head down on the tray and began to cry.

Age 2 years

Edwin was physically well developed and attractive. As he entered the room he looked about, taking in the environment with his eyes, occasionally looking at E but when she looked back at him, his eyes went down to test material. When some of the little red blocks fell to the floor, M told him how to get them and how to get back on his chair, which he did. At the end Edwin seemed tired and became a little less cooperative, at one point seeming to be on the verge of tears, but then he climbed onto M's lap and remained in a fairly good mood. It took some time for him to draw a circle but he continued to try, listened attentively, waiting, and again tried to imitate the circle that E made.

M reported that at 11 months he stood and walked; a month or two later he was running, at fifteen or sixteen months he said his first word, "Daddy," and at twenty-one months he was using short phrases. He preferred rough and noisy activities; when restricted he became cross, sometimes yelled in anger or hung his head and whimpered, but was easily comforted. He had had just one or two rages bordering on a tantrum, and a couple of times hit his head on the floor. He now had a habit of taking a kitchen chair, dragging it to the stove, and getting up to see what was cooking in a pot. He climbed in the bathroom to get toothpaste or water and when M sometimes said "No" and tried to remove him, he stood and screamed so that she had to "paddle his bottom." Moving him away from the situation was usually the simplest and most effective method of discipline. When M caught him doing something he was not supposed to do, he looked straight at her but remained silent. There was a suggestion of a long-suffering meekness in her; it turned out that she was troubled by angry feelings toward F, whom she believed had many blind spots in relation to her care of the children.

F believed that the discipline of the children was mainly a problem for M to handle; he stepped in mainly if they were making too much noise; then Edwin would go to his room in anger, or might cry and run to M. F was much more in favor of established rules than M was. He saw Edwin as happy when playing with toys, being loved, or eating ice cream, and angry only when he didn't get something he wanted. F saw his children very little and did not pay much attention to their development. (It was characteristic of a man in his social and economic position to entrust his children to a nanny, and to see them only when dressed up and on good behavior.) He was resistant to the interview situation, defensive, and either unwilling or unable to share his observations of Edwin.

Age 3 years

Edwin immediately picked up a crayon and made marks with it, then a new crayon and tried out that color. Though his grasp was a little awkward, he had good control of the crayons. Generally he was cooperative, very involved in test tasks but occasionally a bit impulsive as he grabbed for test objects. Then he stood up on a chair, rocked to and fro, and climbed up on the table. His fine and gross motor abilities were excellent. At home, he played in his room, often asked M to read to him, and liked to help her and watch her work. When on occasion she left him to do other things, he demanded that she come back, and if she did not he threw himself on the floor and screamed, but the screaming did not last long and he was easily comforted by being picked up and spoken to gently. When he was obstreperous, M's firm voice was enough to calm him, sometimes she spanked him through his snowsuit, which he knew was a reminder for him to behave. Though he chided her for it, she felt he was justified. She also felt that F at times expected too much of his children; her feeling was that they were sometimes rude and annoying, but that their misbehavior was not serious.

Edwin often had opportunities to see his parents naked, as he was apt to come into the bathroom to talk to them while they were bathing. When his brother Adam was born, Edwin was briefly interested in him, then became especially demanding, and after three days told M, "Take the baby back, I hate him." Nevertheless, he liked to help her take care of his brother, with whom he was always very gentle, kissing him when he hurt himself. He had watched M nursing Adam and asked no questions about it, but afterward became demanding. She remembered a time when he had asked why she had no penis and she gave him a book about birth, which he favored for a while and then put aside. He had become more interested in looking at the television, which he watched for about an hour a day. F detested the program but did not forbid Edwin to watch it.

F said that both children were very good when it came to obeying restrictions about dangerous activities. Edwin could be distracted from naughtiness if F looked at him sternly and commanded him not to smile. F's firm voice was usually sufficient when discipline was needed, but on occasion he shook Edwin and put him in his room. He believed that physical intervention that startled a child was what was most effective, and occasionally gave Edwin "a whack on the rear-end." His idea was that at a certain age children get satisfaction out of provoking parents to spank, but the spanking itself was pointless. He disagreed with M's observations of Edwin's sometimes difficult behavior; she saw Edwin as "stable and adjustable," angry about only minor things. He saw M as too conscientious about psychological principles, which he thought were inconsequential. He could not think of anything that made Edwin especially happy, and said that he was unhappy only about having to go to bed, or not getting candy. He saw the past year with Edwin as uneventful except for Adam's birth.

Age 4 years

Edwin was a very well developed, handsome child who on arrival looked around the room, occasionally at E. At first he was shy, lowering his eyes whenever she spoke to him, but as time went on he engaged in all tasks eagerly, smiling all of the time. Although he enjoyed the test situation it was hard for him to sit still, though his restlessness did not impair his functioning. During the cookie break he raced around the foyer, climbed over chairs and tables, stood on his head, and executed somersaults. At all levels he continued to respond with interest and motivation to succeed. On the Stanford-Binet test his estimated IQ was 133.

M said that he preferred energetic physical play, doing acrobatics on an exercise mat, playing ball, and running around a lot. Outdoors he was more apt to join other children than to watch them. When alone on a rainy day he liked to do something with M. He often said he hated F, who was critical of him. M spoke of her own tendency to become impatient and lose her temper; she again candidly explained she was having problems with F, who she felt was too demanding of the children.

Age 4 years, 11 months

Edwin was cheerful and animated. He was easily pleased and broke into an enormous grin when he found any test enjoyable. His speech was exceptionally distinct. His gross motor coordination was also excellent, but his fine motor coordination was inferior. He had difficulty in handling small objects, especially a pencil, which he often dropped inadvertently. With M's help he overcame his initial shyness, and soon he was in a fully agreeable mood. During a break he spoke amiably about his family's trip to the West. After the tests, he amused himself by playing with a ball or selecting a book. When E volunteered to read it to him, he said politely, "No, thank you, I just like to look at it." He maintained a fine balance between cooperation and self-assertion. Although he enjoyed the test experience, he found it hard to tolerate the inactivity that it entailed. When not physically occupied, he fidgeted, rocked back and forth, tilted his chair, and fiddled with extraneous materials. After testing was over he engaged in very energetic play for well over half an hour, chasing a ball around, hopping, doing somersaults; he also engaged in some handling of his genitals. He found it difficult to admit failure only at the WPPSI Block Design item. At other times, he admitted that he was guessing. When asked the number of items in a dozen, he replied, "twelve," then with a mischievous twinkle in his eye he added, "I just guessed at that."

M had a warm, engaging smile, and was altogether accommodating in her cooperation and interest. She seemed, however, to be lacking in vitality. It turned out that she was suffering from a bad cold, but this lethargy had been noted in previous contacts and did not appear to be situational. She consistently showed interest in Edwin's well being, was always ready to assist him, and never intruded on his activity. E was struck by her considerate treatment of the child, her pleasant tone of voice with him and her steady show of affection, which Edwin reciprocated.

He was restless, yet extremely cooperative throughout the test session. He tackled difficult items eagerly and found rewarding not only their challenge but also the fact that he could succeed at them without assistance. He was most happy when engaged in physically energetic activity.

M reported that Edwin's self-toileting had been maintained, but he sometimes got sleepy and refused to urinate. Occasionally he got up at night and went to the bathroom by himself. He now had his own room with an intercom system. M tried to wait for F to come home before putting Edwin to bed and often was annoyed because F repeatedly came home just at the children's bedtime, or sometimes much later with no explanation. Edwin had a nightlight on his bureau, took to bed several of his animal toys, and his special blanket. On occasion he woke up asking for water and for M to stay with him. At such times she spent the night on the empty bed in his room, and also stayed there any time when he was not feeling well. In the morning he brought his blanket to his parents' room and got into bed with them. If F was tired and wanted to stay in bed longer, M got up to be with Edwin. He could and did go to the kitchen and get cookies for himself, and bread, which he spread with mayonnaise. He did not dress himself. He usually bathed with his brother, sometimes with F.

Edwin had started a bug collection during the summer and preserved it for next year. He was interested in nature and animals. As F liked to hunt and fish, he encouraged Edwin to talk about conservation and pollution. In the country, Edwin collected rocks and tadpoles; in the city, he loved to go to the Museum of Natural History with F. He asked many questions about the insects and animals he had seen in the park or on television. M felt that he preferred to work in clay and wood rather than paint. He didn't like to take directions, though he was willing to let F instruct him in the use of tools. On weekends, F often took the children on outings. Edwin was closest to M and scared of F because of F's authoritarian ways. M believed he was typically either sociable or utterly frustrated; when frustrated he became angry but tried to control himself and was sad only when M scolded him. Edwin had no fears except of being yelled at, was stubborn about television and about Adam's interference with his activities. His bad moods never lasted long. M resorted to discipline mainly for rudeness or fights with his brother. Sometimes she gave Edwin a "whack" on his bottom, and once hit his fingers after he hit Adam in the face. She knew that hitting was not the best method of discipline, but it was effective. She added that F was "going mad" because he thought that M's discipline was "impossible," that is, not enough. She could tell by the expression on Edwin's face that he had done something that he felt was wrong, such as drawing on the wall, or pushing Adam. During the past winter he had fibbed at times, projecting blame on someone else. M encouraged him to admit a lie, explaining that there was no reason for it. She felt that he had a strict conscience, expected other children to behave decently, and was angry if they pushed Adam around. M and F had a few arguments that troubled the children, Edwin in particular. F continued to feel that M should be a firmer disciplinarian, while she continued to feel that Edwin should be allowed to go to his own room "to blow off steam." She tried to let the children settle their differences on their own, but F was apt to make them stand at attention and confess; she had not known he would be so moralistic. She was as usual very agreeable and approached the interview with seriousness, but seemed tired and somewhat depressed. Her reports were always relevant, well organized and interesting. She again implied that things between her and F were not smooth sailing, but volunteered no detail. E was hesitant to probe for more information in view of M's past reluctance to speak of marital problems.

F's reports were brief: he mentioned Edwin's visits to the dentist, his special shoes, his excellent appetite, his self-toileting and bedtime routine, and that F sang a song to him at bedtime. Edwin still liked to take four or five stuffed animals and his blanket to bed with him. He accepted M's choices of clothing, bathed with his brother, occasionally took a shower with F, and had not asked questions about sexual differences. F had observed no doctor play and would not be troubled by it; he planned to provide religious training later. He told at length about the television programs that Edwin liked, how long he watched, how he sometimes joined F to watch a ball game, how he loved to go to the zoo or the aquarium and was still collecting bugs. F spoke enthusiastically about the model rockets he had built with Edwin. The two children usually got along pretty well, and he described Edwin's usual mood as "total exuberance." At first F said he had not observed sadness in Edwin; then remembered having seen him sad when he saw an animal that was hurt. He was angry when he didn't get his own way. At such times, he hit, yelled, shouted, "I hate you," ran to his room and slammed the door, but he got over these outbursts quickly.

The interview lasted barely an hour. F's brief reports contained none of his earlier complaints about Edwin's "babyishness" or M's over-protectiveness. He had never been especially observant of his children, but in the past he had shown some awareness of Edwin's individuality. On this day, he might have been talking about someone else's little child, rarely seen, and then only when on good behavior.

Observation at School: Age 5 years

Edwin appeared to derive tremendous pleasure from school. Generally he was in good spirits, smiled incessantly, and squealed with laughter whenever anything struck him as funny. He was also highly energetic, as he raced rather than walked from one place to another, seeming to find it painfully difficult to sit still during structured activities. He showed real enjoyment of his skills and called other children's attention to some things he had built. T said that he was more than willing to enter into group activities, which seemed to the observer to be an understatement, as he not only approached group activities eagerly, but also behaved disruptively. During group discussion he blurted out answers without first raising his hand. When another child found it hard to tell the difference between Tuesday and Thursday, Edwin jumped up, ran to the calendar, and called, "I can tell the difference! There's no 'H' in Tuesday." This excessive need for attention also appeared in his clowning behavior during group activities, and by his either shouting, giggling or making fatuous comments. He seemed to be always calling attention to himself, frequently commenting about other children's responses, and uttering dramatic shouts to emphasize something scary or dangerous. When another child made an innocuous statement he repeated it, then giggled uproariously. His need to be heard was finally manifested by his clamoring to be called upon by T only to have nothing to say. For example, at the end of Show and Tell, he waved his hand wildly, was finally told that he might have a turn, ran to his cubby and returned with nothing in his hand. When T asked what it was that he wanted to show and tell, he just shrugged. Similarly, when the T selected a record to play for the children during rest period, he shouted, "I know what record it is!" Told by T that he might guess, he shrugged his shoulders and said, "I forget."

Edwin's response to social demands was poor. Throughout the day he avoided cleaning up and instead talked and giggled to another child. Even when T approached and asked what he was doing, he continued to talk to his friend. Only when T shouted his name did he grudgingly replace some pieces of play equipment, immediately racing back to the slide to play on it. This poor response to social demands also appeared in his restless and disruptive behavior during rest period. Rather than lie quietly on his mat as T repeatedly asked him to do, he crawled around on the floor, kicked his legs in the air, talked and giggled loudly with another child -- preventing others from resting. His manners were somewhat improved during snack time, when he was quiet and ate in an orderly way. This improved behavior may have stemmed from inhibition in the presence of T and O (observing clinical psychologist), both of whom sat at a table with him. His fine motor coordination was exceptionally poor: he gripped small objects loosely and awkwardly, appeared to be painfully aware of his lack of competence and avoided engaging in fine motor tasks. Early in the day, he walked to a table where some children were involved in an art project. With a look of disdain he exclaimed, "Yuck," and walked away from them. He never approached any Ts, and when he found himself unavoidably in their presence, he behaved in a shy, retreating manner, responded to their questions in a soft, hesitant voice, and once when a T spoke to him he actually turned his head away from her.

One of Edwin's strengths appeared in his ability to amuse himself. During free-play time, he busied himself at some activity with purpose. During a lengthy pause between activities, while other children simply waited for another activity to be introduced, he went to the bookshelf, picked out a book, stretched out on the floor and read it with a friend. Later, as most of the children wandered about the yard looking for something they might do, Edwin went directly to the jungle gym and climbed it quickly and excitedly. His gross motor coordination was superior, and his large physical movements were quick, deft and executed with evident self-confidence. It seemed that when he liked an activity, he attended to it with care. He listened attentively to the French teacher, was very well behaved when she read a story to the children, sat perfectly still and listened, but some of the time he seemed bored and was restless. For a long Show and Tell period, he walked about, fidgeted in his seat, made irrelevant comments to T, giggled without provocation, made silly faces and gestures, and either talked to, poked at, or nudged children seated next to him. Time and again T found it necessary to remind him to be quiet or to leave others alone. She told E that Edwin became inattentive when a subject was not interesting to him and sometimes became "violently silly," needing to be removed from the group.

O described his interactions with children as didactic, competitive, disruptive, excited, silly and aggressive. He appeared to want to be an undisputed leader in the classroom. For example, after having driven a large toy truck around the room for several minutes he abandoned it. Then, noticing two other children playing with it, he raced over to them yelling, "Get off." When they did not, he pushed one of them aggressively. On several other occasions when another child wanted to have some blocks Edwin quickly said, "I'm going to need most of these. You guys can have the rest." Surprisingly, the other children did not challenge him and began to play together. When Edwin noticed this, as if jealous, he suggested, authoritatively, "Hey, we can make a rocket—Bob and I. Not you guys or girls." When the children did not respond he persisted, "Only Bob and Brook can be on my team!" Bob looked up briefly and said, "I don't want to be on your team." The other children ignored him. Edwin, obviously disconcerted, watched the children build a rocket with increasing annoyance and when they finished their rocket, said derogatively, "Hey, that's not a very good rocket."

Edwin's behavior in school was puzzling; he appeared to be most contented there, though he was hyperactive and seemed to be using school to very poor advantage. He attended well only to activities that he himself found interesting. T reported that his behavior had changed greatly over the course of the year. For the first few months he had been exceptionally shy and retiring; at about Thanksgiving he began to feel at ease and had become "gregarious, outgoing and wild." At the beginning of the year, he also had a special friendship with a girl in his class and shared all his work and play materials with her. In the past month he had had nothing to do with her and was now seen to be playing only with boys. T spoke spontaneously about Edwin's wealth of information; he was well versed in a number of subjects and was eager to contribute a lot of information to class discussion about space, nature, and foreign countries.

Age 6 years

Edwin's grooming was casual. His lips were chapped and his hands were very dirty, almost black in color (after school). His speech was intelligible, his vocabulary mature. In the M-C (mother-child) play, one sensed warmth between the two and an ability to interact smoothly and with pleasure. He enjoyed most of the WISC testing, engaged in spontaneous conversation with E, and was sober except for an occasional smile, but he rocked in his chair, almost falling off, picked his nose, and played with a tissue. Tension was evident as he placed both hands in his pants next to his genitals for some length of time, or ran both his hands together across the edge and the underside of the table; or moved his hands about in swooping motions, pushing them against the table. At the same time, he talked quietly to himself, whistled, asked rhetorical questions such as "How should it go?" and hummed. He never avoided difficult tasks.

Edwin still took his blanket and several stuffed animals to bed with him and sometimes wanted a light on in his room. He needed urging to dress for school, and sometimes wet his underpants slightly. At M's encouragement he now did more things with F. Edwin had become somewhat distant from M since the birth of another brother, though he became solicitous towards her when the parents had arguments. M told him to come to her when problems within the family arose, but thought he could probably work things out amicably with his friends. He enjoyed scientific toys and projects, being read to, reading aloud to M and building models. When alone, he attended to his growing seedlings, made models, set up soldiers, or took out a game he could play with himself. M thought that he would soon outgrow his excessive interest in action stories, space shots and other scientific events and had now developed an interest in maps. He was more self-assertive than he had been a year ago and difficult at times, especially with F who was "authoritative." Then he made an effort to control himself by defiantly going to his room for a time. When frustrated he withheld tears as long as possible, and needed discipline mainly for getting angry and out of control with family members. M was feeling a little worried about these outbursts and tried to divert his attention with, for example, an early bath or a game he liked or by having him help her with something. About three times a year, she would lose her temper and spank him ("just one swat"). Then always tried to talk with him about it. He became angry if he didn't get his way, or felt unjustly treated. He had most trouble when angry at F. M thought his fear of losing his F's love prolonged his outbursts; he had temper tantrums once or twice a week stemming from annoyance with F's strictness. He typically covered up sadness; when, for example, his parents went away, he would say that nobody loved him and then try not to cry. M now divulged that F's frequent absence from home in the evening was the result of a compulsive addiction to gambling, which he had only recently revealed to her. She then referred to F's short temper, expressed frustration about his intractability, and revealed her own continuing need for tranquilizers. She volunteered that she did not plan a divorce.

F said that Edwin entered kindergarten with some resistance to the routine, having problems with written work because he was left-handed, but enjoying social relationships. He bathed by himself or with Adam, and sometimes took a shower with F. He always took his blanket to bed with him and F read a story and sang to him at bedtime. All of F's reports were blandly positive. E heard nothing about Edwin as an individual, only generalities about his interests and accomplishments, though F noted that he considered Edwin to be impatient, adding that he probably expected too much of Edwin. Edwin reacted to frustration with anger and tears, and might respond by going to his room and shutting the door. He needed less discipline now than formerly for disobedience or aggressive behavior. F often lost his patience and yelled at him. He believed that hitting and spanking were not effective and could not remember when he had last spanked Edwin. He objected to reporting what made Edwin happy or sad and facetiously listed things like eating ice cream, watching television and going outdoors. He didn't know when Edwin might feel guilty about anything, and objected to the assumption that every child might sometimes feel guilt. He thought Edwin was "in control of his own destiny." He answered as much as possible in monosyllables, and always in a way to validate Edwin. He asked no questions and the interview was completed in an hour.

Observation in School: Age 6 Years, 1 month

The T spoke of Edwin positively in most respects, especially socially, but added that he was occasionally disinterested in group activities. In the rooftop gym, it took quite a while before he was able to engage in any of the games. He showed even less spontaneity during a rehearsal of the class play. A more basic weakness in his functioning seemed to lie in his dislike of academic work, perhaps because he was left-handed.

Age 7 years, 1 month

Edwin was tall and sturdy. His speech was excellent. M was as usual friendly and articulate. As the tests went on, he became restless, shifting in his seat and standing up occasionally, though fully attentive. On the Picture Completion test he received a much lower score than he had a year before. For example, when shown a picture of a cat whose whiskers were missing, he said nothing was missing; it was the same when he was presented with a door whose hinges were missing. He was challenged by the Block Design test, smiled often and made expressions of amazement and joy at his successes. During Verbal subtests he scratched both sides of his head simultaneously, several times put his finger in his mouth, stood up momentarily to stretch his arms, and put the pencil down the front of his shirt. He was fully at ease in his ability to engage E in conversation, and approached all items diligently, indicating a high motivation to achieve. He spontaneously related the WRAT items to his schoolwork. Near the end of the test he was tired, and indirectly indicated that he wished testing were over. Nevertheless, he kept trying to behave appropriately and remained friendly. His WRAT reading score was converted to a grade of 3.8, spelling to a grade of 2.0, and arithmetic to a grade of 2.6. He worked diligently and guessed on many of the reading words, at times using a phonetic, syllable-by-syllable approach.

M noted that he was striving to develop his athletic abilities. She thought he enjoyed challenges but would never be the brightest in his class, and had some uncertainty about his placement, probably because he had begun the year slowly (he was found to be left handed), though his work was gradually picking up. He did not complain about school, but M noted that some of the work was tiring and dull for him. He was excited about music and assemblies, but hated French. Since the Christmas holidays he had shown more interest in reading, but not writing. Recently, he had shown more interest in reading outside of school.

The children now ate breakfast together, sometimes with F present. Edwin was often restless at meals and might wander away from the table. Sometimes his attention was diverted because he was interested in so many things and needed time to do them. In the morning, he dressed himself completely, managed his toileting and might walk the dog. He was reluctant to get dressed and had trouble tying his shoes and his necktie (school required formal dressing). He chose his own clothing.

Relationships among the children had calmed down, especially as Edwin realized his siblings got into as much difficulty as he did. Edwin was generally easy to get along with. M had gone through a period of thinking he was hyperkinetic because he would run through the apartment doing his exercise, often wearing himself out before his bedtime, so that M began to serve supper to the children at 5:30. Edwin had become easier to deal with recently, but still needed to be shown a lot of loving, especially physical love. Asked what might put him into a bad mood, she said her raised voice would do so, or sometimes he was angry at one of his siblings for supposedly stealing a friend, or at F. He was often bothered by anyone who screamed or got mad; he didn't like loud noises. He didn't like it when M yelled at any of the children. No one liked it when F got mad, and recently, Edwin, in response to F's anger, had become very dramatic and said that he was going to run away.

His favorite television programs were about animals, such as those by Jacques Cousteau and Walt Disney. During the school week he watched television for just an hour a day. Often that hour stretched out, but in the country he woke up and went outdoors and did not watch television. He had an enormous bug collection, was interested in other aspects of nature study, caught frogs and snakes, and liked to watch nature shows, learn about Indians, and read about animals in National Geographic. In the summer he might garden. He showed interest in the environment, and had discussed soil erosion during visits to the park.

The family had not discussed social problems much; Edwin was clearly more interested in natural phenomena. His only present ambition was to learn to ride a bicycle. M noted that he had an infectious giggle and made friends easily. She first said that she didn't know what he disliked about himself, then said that he felt he did more things wrong than his brothers did. He might "explode" in certain situations, but M noted that this never lasted long. He used to say, "It's always my fault," and there was some truth in it, but in the last half year the situation had improved and he no longer felt singled out or unfairly blamed. He had needed discipline for punching, throwing things, and sometimes slapping or being rude, though he was never rude to M. She knew that Edwin received much discipline at school, and that it was hard for him to be less active than he was. She felt he had achieved about the usual amount of control that could be expected of a 7-year-old with respect to his temper, his "explosions" and his storming into a room. After such occasions, he'd send her little notes, saying such things as, "Mum's a bum." She again noted that their home situation was not ideal. His Ps did not get along well in many ways; this had to be affecting the children's behavior. Edwin was learning to cope with their many arguments, but still was sad if he knew that M and F were arguing, and needed many reminders that he was loved. If there was an argument about him, he tried to establish his position, and became quite frustrated if he felt he was not being understood. Though frightened by F's periodic anger at the children, the intensity of his own anger was sometimes quite violent. Such anger occurred a couple of times each week, then he became very tight internally, stiffening but not speaking.

He usually could admit when he had done something wrong, though out of shame, he sometimes lied that it was somebody else's fault, even the dog's. At such times, M took him aside and spoke to him until he admitted it. She worried about his tendency to become explosive, feeling that she was perhaps too watchful, but didn't want Edwin to be fearful of punishment or to lie as a result. She made plain that she didn't want the lying to become a device of self-deception for Edwin the way it was for his F. In the present, he chewed his fingernails and often sucked one or two fingers. His only discontent at present was about the situation in the family. M told him that she and F were not going to get divorced and Edwin didn't think they would, but F was difficult to deal with. There were long periods in Edwin's early life when he would wake up in the night and M would sit up with him and caress him, feeling sure that tensions within the family affected him. M believed his outgoing nature, his sense of humor and the things he noticed about other people showed him to be a very aware person. He took notice of clothing, of a small bug that might appear on the street, of women being pretty. She felt he needed most to cultivate more his capacity for having a sense of satisfaction with himself. She felt that if he could develop more of that satisfaction it wouldn't matter so much if he weren't the best swimmer or baseball player. She didn't want him to feel that he had to conform to ideals, and she thought that "he is very nice the way he is." M said she had a good deal of information about young children, but never really enough. She could always know more; most of her information she said came from involvement in our project. When Edwin as a baby cried all night, SB suggested that M stay with him and touch his cheek softly. Such advice (given in no other case) helped her very much; she said it was difficult to come by in books.

M said Edwin was outgoing on the surface and appeared to be happy-go-lucky, but appearances, she well knew, were not always accurate. In an aside, she made a comment to the effect that although F appeared to be a happy-go-lucky fellow, he was really far from that. She added that in Edwin's infancy F was often away from home for a day or two and so did not play with him a great deal. In this lengthy interview, E found M to be a very well-informed, concerned parent whom it was pleasant to interview, yet her situation seemed to be very unhappy, offering her limited alternatives.

Tests, Age 18 years

Edwin had thought that his time with us would be spent in SAT-like tests, but hoped it would be spent on "more fun things, like the ink blots." He was a very willing test subject, worked hard, and appeared to get great pleasure from his successes. As measured by the WAIS-R he received a full scale IQ of 131. An ease of verbal expression characterized his responses. He responded with humor at the Picture Arrangement stories, finding contexts having to do with social attunedness easy and enjoyable, and achieved perfect solutions on all of the puzzles. His high expectations for himself were evident throughout. The projective tests suggested a contradiction between personal freedom and responsible adherence to external expectations, and a pervasive feeling that interpersonal relationships might not be successful. Thought processes bore the mark of a creative person with a good ability to organize and integrate.

His easy articulation on the Rorschach tests gave a picture of a young man who was quite knowledgeable, well versed in cultural arts and very responsive to the creative possibilities of the blots presented to him. Upon further scrutiny, E became aware of an excessive ease in his thinking, which bespoke internal stress and suggested the possibility of inner discomfort defended against by an intellectual stance. His Rorschach responses suggested internal anxiety and feelings of disaster. These distancing attempts were defensive maneuvers to cover internal stress that was often too painful for him to confront. The TAT stories suggested difficulties in his relationships to his family, and tension associated with his own identity. From a passive aggressive stance against parental expectations, he moved to issues of identity and being different, with a degree of empathy for the paternal role. To picture 9BM he said, "This is the life. A bunch of hobos. They're crashed. It looks like hobo is wasting time. Whatever they're dreaming about, their life is simple. They don't seem to worry about anything. They like their life. I don't know what will happen. Their life is a day-by-day life. They take things as they come." The story seems to evolve from depression about lost relationships and loneliness.

Diagnostic statement

Edwin was a young man of superior intelligence and clearly advanced capabilities. It was difficult to tell if there was some learning weakness in his history, but there was a greater suggestion of emotional unrest, particularly regarding conflicts between loyalty and autonomy, pleasure and responsibility. His responses suggested a latent depression, internal seething, and some indications of allowing pleasure to overwhelm his capacity for monitoring his performance. Difficulty arose in modulating his feelings, which appeared to be dealt with defensively by his intellectual and cultural sophistication. Though he showed many cognitive and emotional strengths, one sensed that he was internally more stressed than his outward appearance suggested.

Interview, Age 18 years

Edwin was an engaging almost eighteen-year-old young man who arrived a bit late after a difficult drive for which he apologized, yet he was proud of having negotiated a severe snowstorm to keep his meeting with me, and refused train and bus fare. He was willing to share his present occupations and to speak of his school and vacation plans. He denied having ever had any real school problems, saying that he was repeating the ninth grade only because he hadn't worked hard enough. He was happy about nearing the last year in his prep school, felt he was doing well and hoped to achieve a B average. He said he hadn't worked much because he enjoyed sports and friends more, came out with a C+ average, which he didn't feel was bad at all. At present he enjoyed American History in which he received a B. His best class had been pre-Calculus. Considering that he felt he had done well enough, it was surprising that on the SAT he got only a 450 in Math and a 500 in English. He participated in extracurricular activities only during the present year, volunteered time as a companion in a home for the elderly, and did some tutoring in a high school. He didn't know what he might be interested in doing in the future, and had thought of Marine Biology and Oceanography, after having seen television programs about them. Really, he said he thought he would like a desk job someday. He had a number of good friends, whom he described well. He had also had a friendship with a girl for two years and saw her a great deal. In free time, when he had no obligations, he might pick up a magazine, or maybe write letters, or probably catch up on sleep. He liked to look at science magazines, especially about mechanics and physics, but had never been particularly interested in reading, usually preferring to go out with friends. Best of all he liked being with people. As a last resort, he might perhaps read a mystery or a spy story. F was involved in a business concern that sounded shaky, he really didn't understand much about it, probably because F did not take much pride in his work. M had been a teacher in a private school. His parents never went out anywhere. F might go out, a little more than M, or might play bridge or go to his club once in a while, but mainly kept business appointments. On weekends F worked out in the yard and did reading of all sorts.

As a result of F's addiction to gambling, there had been great tension in the home. Often Edwin left the table in anger, and there were big fights when F would blow up at him for no reason at all. He had difficulty with his brother Adam who also often fought with F. Adam lacked ambition, had rowdy friends with whom he drank beer, and did most things haphazardly. "He just tries to be cool." As Edwin went over the whole family's relationships, it appeared that now each one got along with the others except for F and Adam. F, he said, loved children, loved all the children's friends, and enjoyed sports, fixing things, and seeing old friends. Edwin knew that his parents had many times thought of divorce, but believed they never would, as they did need each other.

Edwin described how he got irritated when bored and very fidgety when he didn't have anything to do, describing boredom as the worst feeling he could have. He was irritated by what he deemed to be inappropriate public behavior, and became frustrated when on a test he got a mental block or couldn't think of something, like a math formula. When that happened, he daydreamed for a while, then came back to the subject. He got disappointed when he tried to do something especially good for someone and failed at it; certainly he got upset when people yelled at him when he didn't do something right. He had become angry at M when she jumped to conclusions and tried to influence him. He used to have temper tantrums as when F got upset with him for nothing. Questioned about his anger, he told that he punched through a wall, but that it was only a plasterboard in the attic. He had also twice put his foot through a wall in their country house. He was most happy when with friends and listening to music, and when he could be carefree and do whatever he wanted, like going off in the car for a while, just free.

He liked about himself that he could get along with people very well, liked helping people at school and was proud of his skiing. He thought his conscience was quite lenient. He could name no reason for ever having been concerned about anything or worried about anything at all. About his grades he said again, they had been fine, always a C+, which was good. The only habit he could think of was nail biting, which he said bothered everyone else but not himself. He had no fears, but always had dreams of falling. He could think of no way in which he had ever wished to change himself. He believed that children needed a mixture of care, discipline, and free time, and that adolescents needed guidance, care, and free time. He hoped that he might have three children, but because it would be too hard financially, probably he would actually have only two— not one, because an only child is not good "because you need someone to fight with." He said he had gained knowledge about the Ten Commandments and how important they were from the fellowship at the church. He said, "Whoever wrote them down was pretty clever because they cover everything." He said he believed in the death penalty, adding, "Of course they could be falsely acquitted," realizing this was an error when I brought it to his attention. He did not believe in a higher drinking age. "If a young man can fight for his country and vote at eighteen, there is no point in raising the drinking age. Anyway, people drive fast between seventeen and eighteen, when they first begin to drive." He appeared not to think deeply about rules for young people, though he spoke strongly for abortion. He was for ERA and against MCPs, which I learned meant Male Chauvinist Pigs. He felt that every one in high school should do some kind of civil service and through doing so could get some idea of what they'd like to do with their lives. He said he would like to change society in a way that would make for less unemployment and poverty. He didn't think there would be a nuclear war "unless a terrorist got at the button and pressed it." The big powers didn't really want war, as it was a disaster for everybody. "If there were a nuclear war, the lucky ones would be killed right away." Politically, he was very conservative.

He wanted to obtain and hold a steady job, mentioning again that he would like a desk job. He wanted to make money, and thought inventing something would be a good way to do it. He had thought sometimes he'd like to be an architect, but he couldn't draw well, so that would be "a kind of hit or miss profession....If you blow one job, you've got a bad name and you can get no further." He spoke of other ways of getting rich, and of how much he would love to fly, and to try both parachuting and hang gliding.

Clinical impression

Edwin was clearly very intelligent and displayed a sincerity and integrity that made him very likeable. He had, however, become somewhat superficial in his thinking and his interests; he seemed to have no ambition and very limited self-criticism. His interest in the world at large seemed lacking or naïve. It seemed that he was managing to get along by a policy of "no sweat." It was as if, over the years, he had traded intellectual or thoughtful concern for freedom of spirit. Consciously and unconsciously, he avoided feelings of conflict—this may have been his way of trying to be less hurt by the family turmoil related to F's gambling. He had lowered his standards for himself, but still appeared to be a good citizen, entirely friendly and with good social judgment and a certain balance in his personality. If he could find work to do that interested him, he said he would feel quite satisfied with his life, though he might lack fulfillment. His saying that he would like a desk job suggested that he had already made peace with limited aspirations.

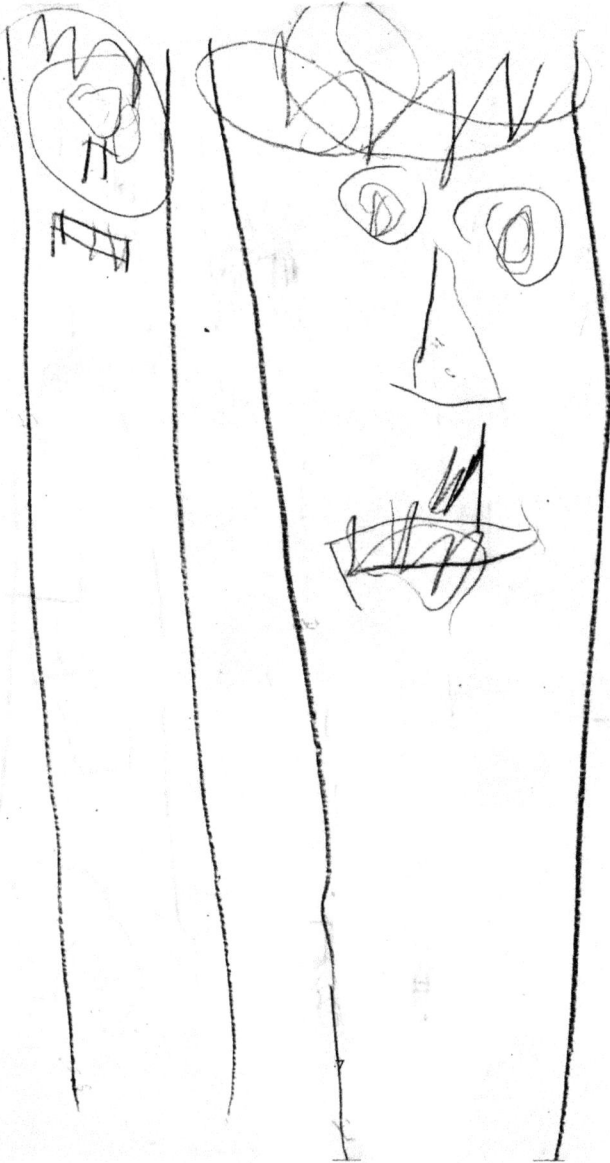

Figure 1: Age 5; His mother and father.

Figure 2: Age 5; His family.

Figure 3: Age 18; "Someone Like Me."

Analysis of Edwin's Drawings:
Exhibitionism, Moderate

Edwin's earliest drawings are somewhat bizarre in their lack of a developed "body" of any sort. His "faces" are perched at the top of long, unbounded rectangular forms. His faces appear muddled and confused, with overlapping circles, more than two at times, representing eyes. Eyes and rectangular mouths full of teeth are prominent in these drawings. Edwin had extreme difficulty drawing in his preschool years, struggling with establishing handedness before settling on left-hand dominance. He was compliant with the task, diligently drawing each of three brothers in ascending order. These drawings indicate aspects of Edwin's early competitive aggression towards his siblings and peers, as well as the palpable presence of aggression in his family.

His drawing of his mother and father point to his acute perception of the power differential in the family, as well as to the constant conflicts between his parents that colored his early years. His mother's face is small compared to his father's, taking up much less space relative to her own rectangular form, while father's face encompasses his whole body. The father's face is noteworthy for a pair of prominently "staring" eyes, and a large, harsh looking tooth-filled mouth. His face dominates the drawing of the parents, demanding that he be attended to, as Edwin's father was a stern and untouchable presence in his life.

In adolescence, Edwin's figure drawing of a male is well-proportioned and neatly drawn. Interestingly, his figure stands in a confident, cocky yet unbalanced pose, with one leg bent and off the ground. Due to this instability, the figure balances by gripping a large upright pair of skis, suggesting Edwin's reliance on phallic accomplishments to support his at times shaky sense of self. The musculature of the body is over-emphasized, with wide shoulders and pelvic area in sharp contrast to a relatively small head in keeping with Edwin's eventual dismissal of the importance of intellectual pursuits and adult accomplishments, and his defensive nonchalant stance in the face of anxiety. The face looks younger than the body, though calm and content, seeming to echo his put-on adolescent self-satisfaction. While well-drawn, the image of a boy betrays Edwin's need to inflate himself as a means of protecting against his lingering concerns about his motor prowess and cognitive capacities. In this way, the relative imbalance between head and body in his adolescent drawing speak to Edwin's continuing insecurities about his cognitive abilities and the inflation of his relatively more developed and more showy athletic, physical strengths.

Synopsis

Edwin's early life was fulfilling. His mother, intelligent and loving, appeared to have clear ideas about how to raise him, was consistently empathic, and enjoyed being the subject of our study with Edwin. F's uneven, emotionally distant treatment of Edwin was in strong contrast to hers, which made for some parental discord. F was usually lenient, but when on occasion he objected to Edwin's behavior he had demanded Edwin stand at attention and confess his supposed wrongdoings. F's overemphasis on Edwin's misbehavior, together with the parent's conflicts over F's addiction to gambling, appeared to bring about the child's excessive fear of being blamed.

At ages 4 and 5, Edwin made special efforts to be noticed by other children, sometimes obtrusively, as if to reassure himself of being worthy. Early in his sixth year, he became overbold, almost careless of behavior that he knew was not appropriate, causing other children to withdraw from him. Gradually, his self-esteem was lowered. These conditions probably contributed to his gradual surrender of intellectual aims that he had earlier enjoyed; by age seven he seemed to have lowered interest in schoolwork and was more concerned with social enjoyments.

By eighteen, appearing to have lost his capacity to aspire according to his intellectual and social level, he declared his aspiration to have a desk job. This capitulation, possibly related to a sadness about his F's gambling addiction, was a compromise to protect him from the stress of "making effort and getting nowhere," or making effort that would just be boring. Fenichel (1945) wrote: "The feeling of being bored, at least in its neurotic exaggeration, is a state of excitement in which the aim is repressed... Bored persons are looking for distraction, but usually they cannot be distracted because they are fixated to their unconscious aim" (p 185-186).

Subject 3: Tina: Exhibitionism

BO: 2/2
SES: Lower

M was remiss in every area of infant and child care, and never made any positive statements about Tina except those regarding her physical ability. Scolding or spanking was the only form of effort M made to curb Tina's impulsivity or to help her. Tina developed an excessive need to be looked at and admired.

Confinement visit with M

M was small, plump, dressed completely in black, and wore large, heavy jewelry. Her ashen face and black hair added to her unusual appearance. Her speech and movements were soft and slow. She had no ideas about infant care, and appeared to welcome the interview as a diversion from the boredom of her everyday life. At three days, Tina was moderately alert and accepted breast-feeding comfortably with no irritability. Visual fixation was brief; auditory and tactile responses were stronger. Her movements were normally active, her tension normal, and she fell asleep gradually.

Age 6 weeks

Tina's visual interest in the near and far environment was immediate and intense, yet her long gaze at E's face severely delayed her reactions to test objects. For much of the time she fussed or screamed until she was red in the face, then was unusually active, rolling from one side of the crib to the other, kicking, lunging, and flailing her arms; then suddenly all activity ceased, and she gazed intently at E or at something in the room for almost ten minutes. Then again she was restless, slumped in her seat, and fussed angrily until her face was red. The observed bottle feeding was very disorganized, as M shifted her back and forth from the infant seat to her lap again and again, saying that Tina was almost impossible to feed because she squirmed, arched, ate only a little, and spat out the nipple. She said Tina was most curious about moving objects, and able to play in her playpen for about half an hour if someone was in the room near her, but when alone she screamed until someone would come to her. She had no interest in any objects, sometimes stared at strangers, and spent a large part of every day screaming at the top of her lungs "until she gets her way." M seemed unable to understand how to make her comfortable and continually caused her irritation. Often she let Tina "cry it out," so that she could get her work done. Several times a day Tina made her furious, and once M spanked her for not going to sleep. "No one can figure out this kid," she said, affectlessly. The lack of communication between the two was appalling.

Tina had enormous physical toughness, along with considerable body vigor. When M or E came near her she lunged at them, trying to pull their hair or clothing. At times she was pleasant and had a winning smile, so that E found something endearing about her in spite of her chronic irritability. The screaming that occurred repeatedly was most unusual, and resembled an expression of rage that one might expect to see in an older child. While Tina was tense, high-strung, and very alert, M was slow and sluggish, expressed herself poorly, and seemed vague, as if not really present.

Age 6 months

Tina was thin, wiry, and homely, with unusually alert eyes. She moved very vigorously for short periods of time, lunging, reaching, and making large, almost leaping movements. She would turn over rapidly or kick, then lie quietly for long periods—about ten minutes at a time—looking around at objects in the room with intensity. Again, she was so fascinated by E's face that her reactions to test objects were unusually delayed. Then she was restless, slumped in her seat, and after the Mirror Presentation test shrieked loudly for no observable cause. E could not pull her to a sitting position because she became so rigid that she did not bend at the waist and so was pulled to standing. M said that she cried a great deal and had to be held, rocked, and fed on and off and all day. During feeding she usually squirmed, arched, took only a little milk, and spat out the nipple. M tried to feed her in a standing position, still shifting her back and forth between the infant seat and her lap. As she tried to insist on Tina's taking more food, Tina screamed until M gave up, trying a final time to force the nipple into the baby's mouth. She had no plans about weaning.

M thought Tina was unusually active, unusually noisy, and in a great hurry to do physical things. She "had a temper," and spent a large part of every day screaming at the top of her lungs, so M often let her cry for periods in order to get her housework done. She spoke to Tina in a sweet but mechanical manner, handled her roughly, and often expressed anger at her for being "such a wretch" and "impossible to deal with." Much of the time, Tina fussed or shrieked angrily, arched, screamed until red in the face, and was extremely difficult to comfort. E had the impression that the baby was in severe pain because of teething, as often after screaming she would put two fingers in her mouth and suck them vigorously. This was her most salient and prolonged activity. She accommodated very well to being held when she first awoke, but otherwise was squirmy and preferred to have only her hands held so that she could stand up straight. Her reactions to object presentations were usually delayed, as she was fascinated with looking at E's face. Her interest in objects had to be re-aroused many times by E, as she grew more and more restless. Her fine motor movements were slower, less smooth, and she took less pleasure in them.

Tina woke at 7:30 am, cried, had most of her breakfast, soon cried again, was given a propped bottle of milk, then fell asleep with it until about noon when she was then taken down to her parents' store where she was given lunch. She accepted all baby foods. Then she might play for a while, but usually was very cranky and had to be held by M or her aunt. After supper she got very irritable, cried a great deal and again had to be held. F refused to hold her, because M and grandmother, "having spoiled her," should do it. M fed her whenever she cried. She slept soundly in a crib in her parents' room, and always awoke in a good mood. When given a bath she used to be so active that she almost slipped out of M's hands and screamed until removed from the water. She no longer screamed in the bath but still disliked it.

Her brother Tom (age 3 years) played with her most, talking to her and giving her toys. M talked to her and bounced her; F liked especially to roughhouse with her. Tina didn't like to be hugged or kissed, and rarely laughed. M thought Tina's irritability was simply "her character," and often had resorted to putting her in a room and letting her "cry it out." Tina had been frightened when M screamed at her, screamed back, and sometimes rocked herself. M appeared to assume that her care was adequate but that "Tina was too much." F played with her if she was good, but when she was bad yelled at M to take care of her. "He's a disciplinarian."

M's reports were vague and often contradictory. She addressed Tina in a sweet but mechanical manner and handled her roughly, often picking her up from a supine position by grasping one shoulder. She seemed quite unable to understand how to make Tina comfortable, and continually caused her more distress than comfort. Several times, M said half-jokingly to E that if E wanted she could have the baby. The difficulties dated from Tina's birth, she said, though she also attributed them to teething, and to Tina's being "spoiled." She hated to think of how Tina would be when she got older, adding that she would be prevented from bad behavior because F would be infuriated and would spank her. Asked if she thought there was anything she or F had been doing that might have contributed to Tina's irritability, M said she hoped it wasn't just Tina's personality, though she believed it probably was.

Age 1 year

Tina was pale, with large red blemishes on her temple and her knees as a result of many falls. Though her body looked frail, her facial expression was mature. Her legs were extremely bowed, probably not helped by very old, worn, dirty shoes. Her outdoor clothes needed mending and could not be fastened. She handled her body excellently. M said "she stood alone at five-and-a-half months, walked and ran at seven-and-a-half months," and never crawled. She loved climbing, had no fear of heights, and could lift herself on a chinning bar and swing her body from it; she stood with unusual erectness, walked and ran adeptly, rapidly, and restlessly, climbed when she could, reached high, bent, pushed, and never stayed in one spot. Now and then she showed an unusual ability to stand very still and look around in a mature way. Her main expression was to squeeze her face up, close her eyes and press her lips together as if to kiss. She was then lovely to watch. Her facial expressions had a quality of composure unexpected in so young a baby. When she did not readily see how to manipulate an object she turned away from it or pushed it away. She vocalized a great deal with much intensity but few modulations. M said that at home she was extremely active, climbing on kitchen appliances, or into the bathtub, or on to her brother's bicycle, falling repeatedly and always recovering quickly. When she resisted being dressed M got very mad, and had to "slap her legs or something like that," after which Tina would throw herself against M in anger. One day when she was trying to get on the dishwasher after F told her not to, she insisted, and he slapped her five times to no avail in spite of her tears.

All her responses to test objects were immediate. She could hardly wait to grasp each one, did so carefully, and perceived relationships between them quickly. It appeared that she could have continued to play at the test table much longer if E had sustained her attention by handing her more objects or talking to her. She then strutted about the room with her bottle hanging from her mouth, which M said was typical; if juice was in the bottle, she occasionally "took a swig" at it. Motor activity absorbed most of her attention; perceptual activity was second, and social activity was least.

M didn't try to keep a schedule, as Tina usually wasn't eager to eat and didn't like sitting, so M waited until she was hungry and then fed her table foods at odd times. She could eat in the high chair, but usually preferred taking pieces of food and walking around with them. She liked her milk warmed and with sugar in it, so M offered it that way. In the morning she had breakfast and played for a while with Tom, then went to sleep at noon with a bottle. In the family store (toys and hardware), she ran about "like a little cyclone," pulling things off the shelves and getting lots of attention from customers. Her best fun was to run around, pick things up, and run off again. She made demands upon M only when tired, hungry, and cranky. When happy she danced, chattered and "went around in circles." She hated having her face washed and being dressed; she would scream, squirm, and try to get away. She responded better when F dressed her because he had once hit her and pushed her down, so now she minded him. "She has more patience with him." She didn't mind if M went out; she might stand by the door and cry briefly. She was curious about everything, but only for a moment. Often she walked out the store door and down the street. M said she was probably going to be a problem because she was so active and had a temper. She used to throw herself on the floor but now when angry she threw herself against M. In the late afternoon she was taken upstairs by her aunt; an hour or two later M went up to fix her dinner, then F came home and played with the children. After their supper M and F went down to the store again, leaving the children with M's sister. Tina "played around" until 10:30, then was put to bed by her aunt.

M was shabbily dressed, her face was pale, her hair disheveled. Her whole manner was toneless, with the exception of mild hand-wringing from time to time. Her dull, circumstantial reporting was reflected in the following verbatim record: "My sister takes them upstairs at five o'clock. I go up and fix dinner a half hour later. Potatoes or vegetables or meat. She eats. I watch her eat. At six my husband comes up. He eats. Then he plays with them." M responded poorly to Tina's fretfulness and rarely looked at her directly, but was always attentive in her own low-keyed way. Asked about Tina's extremely bowed legs, she answered that Tina's legs were just wide apart. She had no worry about Tina's behavior, because of F's "strict character."

Age 2 years

Tina looked delicate, feminine, and was immediately overactive. On arrival she quickly climbed onto M's lap, glanced about, got down again, approached the table with test objects, then grabbed them away from E, saying she wanted to do them by herself. She quickly scribbled with the crayons, showed no interest in the book she was asked to look at, and refused to follow any test demonstrations. She could imitate drawing a line and a circle, made an attempt to draw a cross, then refused most gross and fine motor test items. She quickly built the tower according to E's demonstration, then paid attention only to easy tasks. Confronted with possible frustration she gave up quickly, ignored E's questions, ran about the room taking playthings off their shelves without using them, kept trying to get attention by doing things that she meant to be amusing, and responded to no restrictions at all, leaving M at a loss to know what to do beside threatening to spank her or to isolate her, all to no effect. M appeared to be bewildered and discouraged because spanking was not a reliable deterrent.

Tina did not watch other children at play, M said, but they liked to watch her "because she is such a nut." She liked to clown and make people laugh, but she also bit, kicked, and pulled the hair of much older children, threw her toys about, and showed off. She had to be disciplined for refusing to pick up her toys and making a mess while eating. For example, she threw food into her glass and emptied her juice onto her plate. She refused to do whatever M asked of her, and was spanked every day. Most of M's reporting emphasized Tina's precocious aggressiveness and hyperactivity.

F had tried to punish Tina by depriving her of something or not allowing her to go outdoors. He considered her to be a very unusual child in that she preferred rough and noisy activities, could not bear to watch other children without joining in, and usually tried to control their play. She was stubborn about having her way, never admitted anything, nor could she be distracted when angry or upset; she just had to be physically removed from the situation. In the store, she ripped open packages, threw their contents on the floor, and was repeatedly spanked, in vain. F said he had never seen her exercise any self-control. She still resisted getting into bed, usually falling asleep on the sofa. M then carried her to her own bed; but soon again she awoke and went to her parents' bed. Recently she had developed more fears, did not like to be in a room alone in the dark, cried if older children pretended to be monsters, and feared insects. She treated animals as toys; she walked up to a Great Dane and pulled its tail, and almost strangled a hamster to death. She was especially unhappy when told to stay in her room as a punishment, and "could shed crocodile tears all day long," and was beginning to lie a lot, "while looking you straight in the eye." At first her parents thought her lying was cute; now they were troubled about it. She tried to imitate everyone's acts to prove she could do them better and was sad when guests went away because she loved having their attention. If F showed her a camera she stood against a wall and posed; it was the same when she wore new clothing or curlers in her hair, and she liked to run around the house in the nude. "Basically," he said, "she's an exhibitionist."

Age 3 years

Tina moved slowly into the observation room, avoided eye contact with E, fidgeted, then picked up a crayon and scribbled with it. She refused most gross motor and verbal test items, completing the few fine motor items impulsively, by trial and error. She kept asking where puzzle pieces went without looking at them, or tried to force them into any place. Laughingly, M said that Tina was always having accidents because she tried to do things for which she was too young. "She's a cute wild kid with a big mouth. People get a kick out of her."

F said Tina was quickly bored, jumped from one thing to another, and needed to have people around her to talk with about anything new that was happening or had happened. She reacted to restrictions "violently," lay on the floor kicking, screaming, throwing things, and hitting. He had tried to take a positive approach and be "straight" with her, but she was not straight with him. "She's not genuine." When she did something wrong she tried to soft-talk him, saying, "Kiss me, daddy-mia, I love you a hundred dollars." If he forced her to eat she finally complied and then threw up. He had to spank her several times a day. She mimicked others in order to make fun of them, always tried to be cute, and was content as long as she could do whatever she wanted. She was willing to try everything, but ashamed if caught doing something wrong. F thought she only put on a face of shame but did not feel it, and was spoiled because he bought her whatever she liked, especially dresses because she looked so pretty in them. He believed she would be good at anything she wanted to do, "But if she got the wrong teacher who did not see her individuality, it could ruin her— her individuality would be stunted." He felt, however, that M was much too indulgent. It was clear that he found Tina to be enjoyable and lovable, but had an underlying feeling that there was something quite seductive in her.

Age 4 years

Tina's speech was intelligible but nasal and babyish. She abbreviated words immaturely and had poor grammar. She didn't listen to instructions, carried out most tasks in silence, and when she did speak she directed her words to M. She attacked tasks with exceeding rapidity, was disturbed by the slightest extraneous noise, rocked, fidgeted, jumped out of her chair, ran around the room, and climbed over tables and chairs. She bit her nails, sucked her fingers, pulled at her clothing, made up stories about monsters and drew pictures of them. Her estimated IQ on the Stanford-Binet was 103 (at age three, her estimated IQ on the Merrill-Palmer test also was 103).

M found Tina's behavior exasperating, but when Tina screamed at her she remained passive or made plaintive remarks like, "Oh, God," then kept on giving orders to which Tina never listened. There were frequent conflicts with M about what to wear, for example, Tina's refusing warm clothing in cold weather. Recently she had begun to play with and suck the ends of her hair, especially at night. M said she "told her not to, but did not hit her because of it." Discipline was necessary when she did not listen to directions; giving her a smack brought the desired results. She was happy about getting new clothes or new toys—clapping her hands, jumping, smiling, laughing, looking at herself in the mirror, and telling others to admire her. M's behavior toward E was over-friendly.

F told that in the middle of every night Tina went into her parents' bed; F returned her to her own, but in the morning she was found back in their bed. She dressed herself, usually in unsuitable clothing. F wished she would take more interest in quiet activities like coloring books, but her way was to go through them fast, putting a scribble on each page. She reacted to restrictions with "fake tears," needing to be disciplined constantly, the most effective way being to keep her indoors or in solitude. When happy she jumped up and down, screamed, and took on a facial expression that F could only describe as peculiar. When unhappy, she stamped her feet, pouted, and hid. In anguish she might hit M or Tom, though never F. If caught doing something wrong she was ashamed. F's ideas about Tina had changed. He used to think of her as precocious; now he saw that she put on a good act and had no real creativity.

Observation in school: Age 4 years

Tina's clothes were grimy, her hands filthy, and her hair was in a tangle. She impulsively wanted to attempt as many activities as possible, especially those involving motor skills. She was highly distractible and unable to organize her energies effectively; nor did she make use of help that was offered to her, although she was quick to whine when she encountered even the slightest difficulty. Even when she approached an activity carefully, she worked so rapidly that her project was poorly carried out. When the T offered to work on a puzzle or a game with her, she was able to complete it, but her involvement derived from her desire to secure the T's exclusive attention, rather than from any interest in the activity. Most of her contacts with other children consisted of battles over the distribution of materials. She wrested supplies away from others and shrieked imperiously at them if they protested. There were few moments when she engaged in pleasant contact with other children; mostly she was crudely manipulative; her main attitude toward them was indifference. Her speech with T usually consisted of whining and yelling. When the T suggested that she could remove the turtles from their water tank and look at them, Tina jumped at the invitation and immediately began to push the turtles along the tabletop. The turtles did not react, so Tina pounded the table and screamed at them. When instructed not to do so, she glanced at the T coldly and continued pounding the table in spite of repeated reminders not to. At snack time, when a limited quantity of food was made available, she ran to it at once, screamed to the T, "I'd just like the cottage cheese, not the peaches," downed a bowl of cottage cheese before other children were even seated, and demanded four more helpings. Her haste to eat before the food ran out was so great that she shoved it into her mouth with both hands, and with her fingers scraped up the food she had dropped on the table. She probably had not had any breakfast. Her need for immediate gratification was paramount. At the end of the day she withdrew, rested against a bookcase, and looked miserable. She was not interested in the musical instruments the other children were using, and stayed slumped at the bookshelf, mouthing a bell.

Habits were observed: sucking her fingers, mouthing objects, and nervous play with her hair. Even when pleasantly engaged in individual activity with the T she squirmed about excessively. More unusual were her seductive movements, noted when she approached the male assistant T, with routine wiggling of her behind as she walked. She always spoke in a loud voice that conveyed tension and hostility. She was impetuous, showed extremely low frustration tolerance, and was rarely able to engage successfully in any activity. T said that when she initially joined the group, she had persistently drawn attention to herself by being loud at work time, or by turning lights on and off, or refusing to leave the playground, forcing the T to chase after her. For a four-year-old, Tina's behavior was distinctly infantile.

Age 5 years

Tina was of slight build, plain-looking, pale, with chubby cheeks and a pronounced overbite, exaggerated by her tendency to suck her hair and bite her lower lip. Her clothing was soiled, her hands caked with dirt, her teeth stained and chipped, and she looked malnourished. Her hands and arms were scratched, and there was a large sore on her lower lip. Her voice was high-pitched and abrasive; she spoke so extraordinarily loudly that she was usually shrieking. Nor did she listen to what was said to her. She mumbled, abbreviated words immaturely, her grammar was unusually poor, and there was a vulgarity in her speech that was startling in so young a child.

On arrival (with M) her behavior was bold and self-confident. She walked up to E with a broad smile, and remained self-assured throughout the M-C play; then was reluctant to separate from M. M was very self-conscious, taking a big part in construction of the dollhouse, handing objects to Tina and suggesting where to place them, and was often impatient, annoyed, and critical of how Tina set up the rooms. During a pause in the testing, Tina made spontaneous comments to E, inviting E to visit her at home. After the tests were done, she worked calmly and quietly on her own, but when told by M that it was time to leave, she became obstreperous, shrieked, "No!" then began chanting loudly at M, "Give me the cookies! Give me the cookies!" This impulsivity was the primary sign of disturbance in her behavior. She reached for extraneous test materials, attacked tasks rapidly and restlessly, and when not physically occupied, scowled, rocked, leaned across the table, climbed on it, stood, hopped out of her chair, or ran to various parts of the room. She fidgeted with her hair, sucked on her teeth, pulled on her clothing and frequently scratched her buttocks. She went to the bathroom five times during her stay. Before leaving, she cuddled up next to M, climbed on her lap, took some of the cookies she had saved and gave them to M proudly, then refused to put on the jacket that M was holding for her. On the WPPSI she achieved a full scale IQ of only 88; she had approached all tasks thoughtlessly. For example, when asked what shines at night she said, all too rapidly, "The sun." Asked to draw pictures of her family, she quickly drew a picture of a cousin, then scribbled all over it and said, "I ain't makin' my family, I'm makin' soap first," and drew a tiny figure to represent a bar of soap—probably the use of soap or references to it were frequent subjects in the home. M's hair was long and unkempt, her complexion pallid and blemished, her eyes heavily accented with dark liner. Asked if she would like some coffee, she nodded her head vigorously with tongue extended, in presumed imitation of a dog. At the end of the interview, she was reluctant to leave, and thanked E profusely for having made time to see Tina.

At school, Tina liked best to dress up and to play with the class gerbil. She mentioned children whom she did not like because they were "disgusting and bad and upset the class." Often she was reluctant to go to school, wanting to stay home with M, which M sometimes allowed. Usually M enjoyed having her away for a good part of the day, but Tina was not pleased to be left at school too long, especially in the late winter afternoons, and was often angry when M came late. Tina asked no questions about sexual differences. M thought she had too much interest in other things to bother with sex and babies; she was an extrovert, wanted her own way, and would respond only to threats or punishment. She liked best to do something in the kitchen with M, and she cried when she saw sad movies like Born Free or when she was spanked. When not allowed to wear what she wanted to, she yelled, cried, and might hit M. M thought she was not worried about anything, she was "just afraid to sleep alone." M had never seen her sad. Spanking occurred once or twice a day for disobedience. M thought that Tina's conscience was extremely lenient, adding with a laugh, "She sounds like a terrible kid."

F at first said that "accidents" were negligible, but that Tina had soiled herself a couple of times a week because she postponed going to the toilet, then hid her underpants, so he scolded her and made her soak them and put them into the washing machine. After dinner she bathed, watched television, and went to sleep in her underwear. She awoke nightly to go to the bathroom, then to her parents' bed. If F realized she was there he sent her back to her own bed but she soon returned to theirs. He said the problem was with M, who did not take issue with Tina's behavior. He thought Tina was very conscious of her clothes and hair and looked at herself in the mirror a great deal. She washed her hands but not her face, and needed reminding to brush her teeth. There was a battle every morning about her wanting to wear a dress to school when M wanted her to wear pants because of play on the cold school roof. F hadn't observed Tina's play in the last year, but supposed she might take instruction from another child for about half a minute and then say, "Okay, okay I know," only to go off and do something the wrong way. F said she had ridden a two-wheeler at three and now could roller skate, but was not skillful at any activity requiring perseverance, such as jumping rope. She watched television for about five hours each Saturday morning. She did not care for scheduled shows except for one news report by Dick Cavett (perhaps he provided an echo of her father). She liked to show off her physical achievements, such as shimmying up the ten-foot-pole. In free time she preferred to be in the store with her parents and to play with the dog. The parents were amazed that she had once washed all the dishes. F said that cleaning the kitchen was easier for her than organizing her own room. It seemed probable that being in the kitchen made her feel closer to M.

Age 6 years

M was dressed in purple clothing, a long black sweater, open-toed shoes with straps hanging loosely, and excessive jewelry. She looked worn. She chewed gum quite physically throughout the M-C play. It was not long before the two irritated each other, as when M handed Tina several chairs to which Tina reacted dramatically, saying: "I don't need a hundred chairs!" Sometimes they seemed to boss one another, yet when Tina was having difficulty placing a figure she called out dramatically, "Mama, help!" When the M-C play ended, she continued her acrobatics, often looking at E to see if E was watching her perform her stunts. On the WISC, Tina was distractible, hyperactive and a non-listener. When asked what she might do if a girl much smaller than she started a fight with her, she responded, "I'd beat her up." Asked what she would do if she were to see a train approaching a broken track: "I would stop the train fast—pull the thing back." During much of the test she did headstands and somersaults. Once she hid from E and made faces at herself in the mirror. At other times she played with her feet, sat on them, put her hair in her mouth, or played with a tiny teddy bear. She now slept with M every night. If M tried to make her stay in her own bed, she cried and became cranky, so M felt it was easier to let her stay. The family now had meals together only on Sundays. At home, they watched television while eating. Many times M referred to frowning as Tina's typical angry response. When she lost in a game, she frowned, cheated, changed the rules, accused others of cheating and left the room: she was always angry when she lost, and always boasted when she won.

Bike riding, roller-skating, and playing school were now her favorite activities. M at first said that television was not permitted in the morning until Tina had finished dressing for school, but in the next breath, said she got upset because Tina got too absorbed in the television. She still needed discipline to carry out daily routines, or for speaking too much or too loudly. Sending her to her room was the most effective form of punishment. M slapped her a lot, probably every other day and as always, was passive and apathetic. She complained about Tina's stubbornness and defiance, seeing these difficulties as problematic for herself, but not at all for Tina. As she complained about the high cost of living, she added that she and her husband had considered private schooling for the children, but "that would mean the parents would be spending all their money on the children." F was too busy to be interviewed this year.

Observation in school: Age 6 years

Tina seemed well adapted to the school routine and eagerly included herself in a storytelling session, proudly telling the story of Goldilocks and the Three Bears. When T announced that it was cleanup time, Tina ran to the doll area to help two boys who had been playing there, acting like a responsible adult in a disorderly situation. She appeared to identify with the Ts rather than with the children, and her activities were mainly directed toward recognition by the T. She then spent most of her time alone or with the T, hugging her and following her about. T had noted that she seemed to take pleasure in seeing other children punished or hurt, never expressed sympathy for them, and showed happiness that she was not in their position. She walked about aimlessly, and soon again went to be with the T. O had the impression that Tina was quite content just to be near the T.

Age 7 years

Tina was thin and looked neglected. Her dress was shabby and dirty; her hair rumpled, her lips chapped, her fingernails dirty. She had pimples on her forehead, often wrinkled her mouth or frowned, and had a large Band-Aid on her upper arm, the result of a burn at the kitchen stove. She moved about frequently and restlessly, her motor coordination was excellent, but her speech contained many mispronunciations and much faulty grammar.

M was dressed in dungarees and two sweaters, her fingers were bedecked with rings, and she wore huge platform shoes. Tina immediately asked E for her milk and cookies. During testing she was impulsive, often asking for reassurance. She gave little thought to most of her responses, and often tried to engage E to assist her, or announced that a question was too easy or too hard. Given pieces that would form a horse, she responded quickly, "I can't do it." After a few more seconds she said, "It's too hard—I don't know how—I can't." Her reading score on the WRAT could be converted to a grade of 1.5, her spelling to a grade of 1.2, and her arithmetic to a grade of 1.8. She was able to spell "go" and "in," but several times failed to write the word "cat." Asked about what she disliked at school, she said, "About playing—they should clean up the stuff they play with." The most pleasant thing she could think of was "Clean up the world—clean up the streets and help everybody." The least pleasant thing was "People throwing garbage on the streets." These remarks are reminiscent of her references to soap at age 5. She was restless and distractible, wanting to know if E was married and when she would have the chance to look into E's purse. M said Tina was slow to learn letters, had trouble concentrating and listening, but did good work in reading and math. M had a hard time getting her dressed because Tina wanted to get "dressed up" every day, angering M who thought that Tina had to wear what she was told. Tina now had her own bedroom, but still went to M's bed. She refused vegetables—F had tried to force her to eat them, but as she would then gag and throw up, he no longer did so. M tried to get her to bed at a good time, in vain, as Tina liked to stay up "real late" (after the store closed). M added that Tina didn't like blankets, and in bed liked to put her legs on top of M. It was hard to get her up in the mornings. At breakfast she watched television. On cold days, she liked to go out with just a sweater (a holdover from when she was young and disliked wearing any clothing). She always defended F against M, saying that he could cook better, clean better, and do everything better than M.

Tina's household chores included vacuuming the floors, cleaning her room, making her bed and helping M to dust. M told her she had to help, "and that was that." If she didn't obey, M got mad and told F, who then talked to Tina and she obeyed right away. She had good judgment, although she might rush into something without thinking. Discipline was needed especially about her clothing, as she would change two or three times a day if allowed. Sometimes M had to scream at her to do things, and when that had not worked, M hit her. F did not have to hit her, as Tina could tell from his voice and his look that she must obey him right away. Tina was happy if she got her own way all day long and was sad when she couldn't. She never was angry with F, only with M, then she might scream or cry, "But she does not get intensely angry." Asked how often this happened, M said, "Every day." She didn't like criticism, could not admit wrongdoing, and when angry about being punished, stayed in her room, pouted, and cried. Asked about instances of stealing, M said that Tina didn't have to because she got everything she wanted. She would lie about Tom to get him into trouble, or to protect herself, or she might lie to F about not having had pizza or soda, but she never admitted lies and never showed guilt. Her lying did worry M, although she thought that the children "had to lie" because F was too strict. She was pleased that Tina was aggressive and said funny things. Asked if there was anything she would do differently if she could go over Tina's childhood again, she said she "would try with the vegetables to handle them differently." Asked about the children's moods, she said that both children were happy, didn't get depressed, and laughed easily.

F had no time to come for the last interview. Near the end of the visit, E learned that Tina had to leave the office immediately because F was unexpectedly waiting for her downstairs.

Tests, Age 18 years

Tina was an attractive young woman, fashionably dressed. She was entirely cooperative during the session, but didn't return the Sentence Completion form that she had agreed to do at home. She functioned at an average range overall, and high average in verbal areas. There was much inter- and intra-test scatter to indicate the inconsistency in her functioning. On the WAIS-R, she achieved a full scale IQ of 108. Anxiety, difficulty in concentration, and a tendency to focus on the unessential disrupted her cognitive abilities. She had trouble interpreting the actions of others, which probably interfered with her social judgment. At times she analyzed the tasks into parts and resynthesized them; at other times she relied on trial and error. In structured situations, her thinking was appropriately abstract but often over-personalized. Unstructured situations were stressful for her: she became vague, over-ideational, and tended to retreat into fantasy and confabulations, reasoning from one detail to a whole. She appeared to be experiencing a sense of abandonment and was overwhelmed by feelings of vulnerability; as a result she could become openly paranoid and troubled by morbid thinking. Under stress, her ability to present a socially appropriate façade deteriorated into psychotic thinking. She lacked a basic sense of who she was as an individual; this affected many areas of her life, including sex role identification, long term goals, and loyalty to others. She experienced a pervasive sense of fragmentation. On the Rorschach card V, which is considered to elicit responses to one's self image, she saw "the wolf that's just been killed and someone cut it in half." On card VII, she saw "a leaf that has been torn apart, eaten away on the inside," indicating strong concerns about the integrity of her sense of self. Transparencies in her human figure drawings suggested problems in the area of ego boundaries, causing her to feel inadequate and vulnerable. Pressed by her sense of inadequacy, she withdrew from intellectual challenges, and appeared to feel that if she pursued her own goals she would be abandoned by those upon whom she depended. Her sense of vulnerability was unrelenting, unconsciously causing her to strive for symbiosis with a stronger person. On card VIII she saw "two animals locking into each other, they can move together, there is peace." When she touched, unconsciously, on the theme of symbiosis, she became fearful of the aggressive potential of the figure depended upon, with fears of being consumed and thus destroyed; so that she put a premium on establishing her own space with an intensity that approached the level of a phobia. In response to an authority figure she said, "People praise him... they are bowing to his needs, trying to provide for his every command." She experienced F as a demanding, authoritative figure, and her emphasis on the need for freedom may have represented a flight from fear of domination by him. She was less explicit about M's characteristics but aligned herself with her, feeling that both had been abused and weathered by life. Although she sensed that M was accessible, she was wary of M's anger; she was over-identified with her parents' problems, and expressed concerns about the functioning of her family as a unit. She experienced F as the more unpredictable of the parents, and had greater need to please him though at times she felt oppositional to his demands. She was vigilant to a degree that was inhibiting and had sporadic "lapses," feeling out of control, shameful, and overwhelmed by her poor ability to adapt to emotional stimulation. She showed a tendency to pull away from the past, and was dysphoric because she felt unable to express her affective needs. She had feelings that she was wasting her life, going nowhere. Depressive affect was clearly evident. Although at times she felt like giving up, in a Polyanna-ish way she remained optimistic.

Diagnostic statement

Borderline personality disorder with reliance on projection, splitting, and projective identification.

Interview, Age 18 years

Tina liked elementary school and got along with most teachers though some didn't get along with her, treating her as incompetent. In high school, one teacher had favorites and Tina was not one of them. She had asked for extra help many times, in vain, until one day she followed the T around until she was able to "pin her down," then was finally able to get the help she needed. In high school she received an average of 85, she said. She liked math but never gave it much time. She reported that in her last year her best course was in designing metal jewelry, such as a vest made of copper and nickel—quite heavy, but interesting to make and to look at. From sixth to ninth grade she was on a track team, then began to play tennis. A family friend had shown her a racket, and after watching her with it for a few moments said she would be an excellent player; she had been playing ever since. She took ballet lessons from the fifth to the ninth grades, had taken gymnastics for four years, and was on the swimming team. She liked Shakespeare, "especially *Macbeth*, and *Jane Eyre*." She was now taking a course called *Nature of Language*, "which had to do with the denotation and connotation of words," and she enjoyed Spanish. SAT scores combined were 820. She had been helping her parents in their business—she would have preferred to work at a job away from home but they had not allowed it. She also worked for them during the summers, except for last summer, when she devoted herself to tennis for five hours a day. She planned to go to college for fashion and jewelry design, and hoped to become a professional tennis player.

She had "many, many friends," but not at school "because there were so many different kinds of relationships there that it didn't work out." She had a friend for two years, then they fought. This had happened before. Girls got involved in lots of gossip behind her back and the friendships ended. She avoided lots of people and had many enemies. "Girls just put me down. I'm an individual and don't want to be different." She loved all kinds of music, didn't care much for television, and liked to read but would rather give her time to tennis. At home she had been responsible for many chores. From about age 6 or 7, she had done all the shopping, cleaning, and feeding the dog. Asked if she minded this, she said, "Well, it helped me mature. It's been second nature for me to do it." Pressed to say a little more, she said she wished M were there to do some of these things, but M was always working with F. She and Tom loved each other very much because there was not much love between the parents and children. All of her parents' lives had been devoted to their business. Now they were always telling her what to do, and pushed her as if she didn't know how to take responsibility. Each member of the family cooked for him or herself; they never ate together. The only exception was when they ate out, or had takeout Chinese food once a week.

She had always been tomboyish, which she related to F's having wanted only sons and having brought her up just as he did her brother. He was very upset when she tried to dress like a girl, and a few years ago he had said to her critically, "You're acting like a girl." She wished she had a better relationship with him, but he had not taken her seriously until recently. He used to be very strict, had very bad temper tantrums and really intimidated her. E had to press to find out anything positive about F; after some time she said he was very intelligent and that she liked and respected his opinions. M, on the other hand, was always worried about the children. Tina could tell M everything that was on her mind, which she certainly could not do with F. M would always notice if Tina had something on her mind, and would come to talk to her; everything was good between them. She had gotten sexual information from M—a subject passed over quickly. She wished the family had been "more like a classic kind of family." Her parents had been too business-oriented. They hadn't encouraged her interest in tennis because they thought Tina could do better in designing—they had seen her as a great artist. Their marriage was very good; the family had always been doing things together (all of which contradicted what we had heard before). M always said that Tina tried hard, was very energetic, athletic, and mature for her age. F, in contrast, said she was always stubborn, stern, "and smart because she knew a lot about business."

She was irritated by anyone who was sarcastic or "egotistical;" or people who said, "You can't do that." A friend of her father told her she could be a good tennis player, but not the best. She didn't like that—it was too discouraging. She was frustrated by schoolwork when she tried hard and didn't do well. She was angry with anyone who cheated or lied or stole. She had also been very angry with her parents, who had "no empathy" for her interests and "couldn't find time" when she had tried to talk to them about her interest in college. She liked when she could do things on her own; she was "an individual different from most people my own age, and saw herself as wiser than they about what was going on in the world." She did not like about herself that she had lots of potential in artwork but was not dedicated enough to do it. Her conscience was quite strict. She was always busy with family, school, and her boyfriend. Tina couldn't think of any habits that bothered her, except for some bad eating habits—she used to eat lots of junk food. Other fears had been of the future, school, tennis, and death. F would tell her she had to be rough, and was always putting down women. He said, "All they do is talk about their weight, and beauty parlors." He "put down" M for being overweight, and expressed his low opinion of women when he would say to Tina, "You're changing, you're acting like a woman." M hadn't liked his teaching Tina to do weightlifting and rougher things. M and F were always "tearing in different ways," she said worriedly, without acrimony, but with a certain heaviness.

She would like to have two children, a boy and a girl, and that they should be brought up just as she had been, first in the city, then in the country. She wanted not to force anything on her children, but to let them do what they wanted to do, for example, in business. She herself had to learn on her own a great deal, and thought health and love were the most important things for a child to have. She believed in "free enterprise." If it had not been available, she and her parents would not have been able to do what they had done. She believed in abortion, because "a lot of teenagers need to be able to have it…If a baby was brought up in a no-good home, he or she could turn out to be a criminal, not a good person, or maybe even be insane…And if a kid was brought up with that mother, he would be on an abortion list—I mean a waiting list—and his life wouldn't be good…Someone can be accused of a crime when he had nothing to do with it, and he would be killed for nothing at all," but if there was enough evidence that a person actually did commit a crime, and a lot of first-hand witnesses to it, then probably capital punishment would be right. She would like to change how lots of men were so chauvinistic. Mothers stay home and bring up the children, "like she's lower than him."

Clinical Impression

Tina was friendly and made a pleasant appearance. Her facial features were well formed and she made a good impression, looking in fact rather pretty, but she paid much attention to her abundant hair, which she kept sweeping off her forehead. After a time, I realized that there was little individuality in her facial expression, thinking, or behavior. She had an isolated interest in tennis, and an identification with her parents' interest in business. Her life experience seemed to be narrow, and her reports of not having had friends in school suggested that she was socially disconnected. The family appeared to have lived seclusively, and she may have been more embarrassed by their work (often peddling) than she could let herself realize. Certainly her social life must have been restricted by the amount of housework she had had to do for more than ten years. Her ideas were stereotypic, her vocabulary and concerns limited, and although her grammar was generally all right, it was surprising to hear that for the word "with" she consistently said "wit." There appeared to be a neutralized quality to all aspects of her life, even tennis; for her it was an isolated activity, though it was everything to her, and everything in itself. She tended to boast a little about her practical wisdom and knowledge, yet depression appeared to color all of her comments about her self.

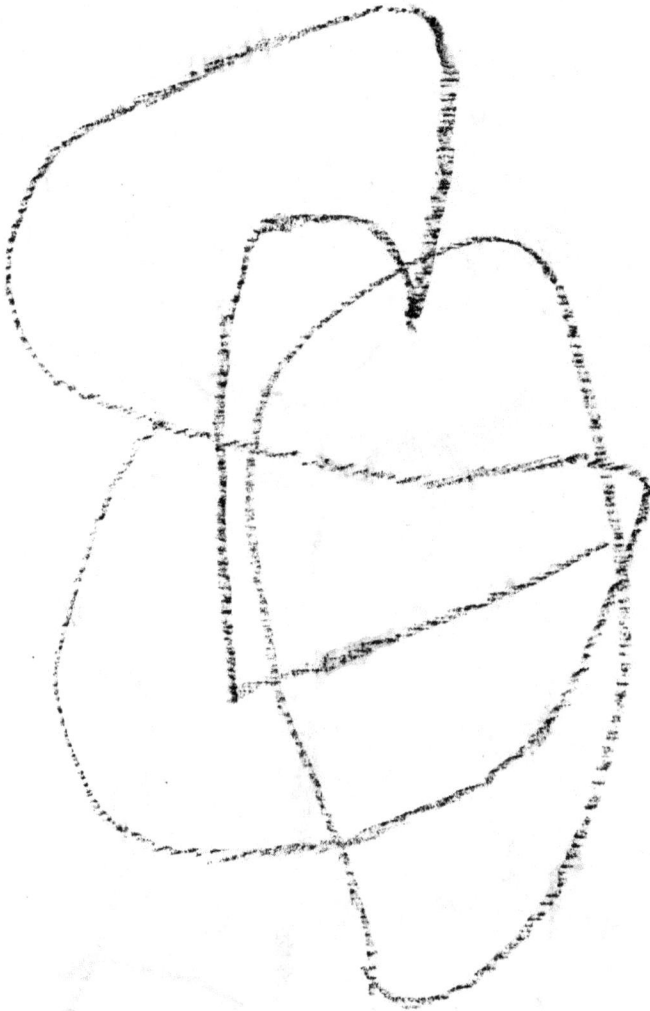

Figure 1 Age 5; Spontaneous drawing of soap.

Figure 2: Age 5; A person.

Figure 3: Age 5; A girl.

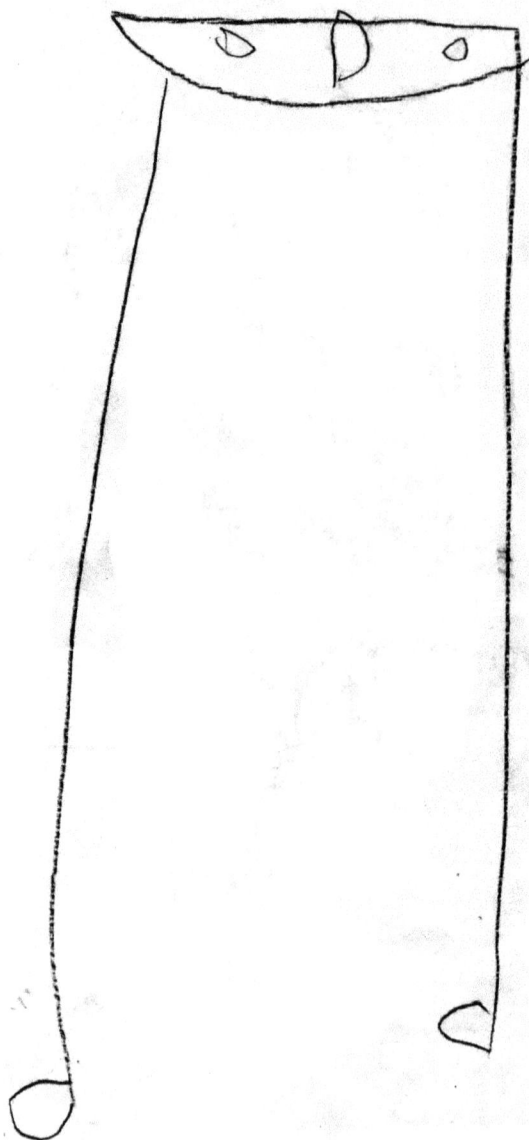

Figure 4: Age 5; Herself.

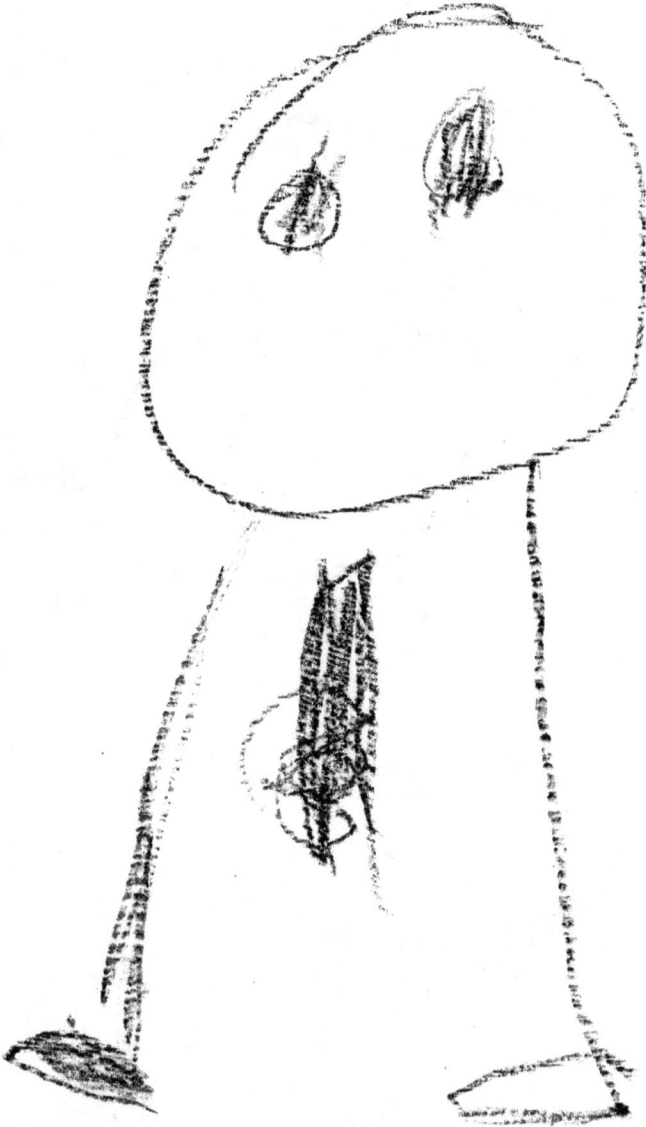

Figure 5: Age 5; Spontaneous drawing of a boy.

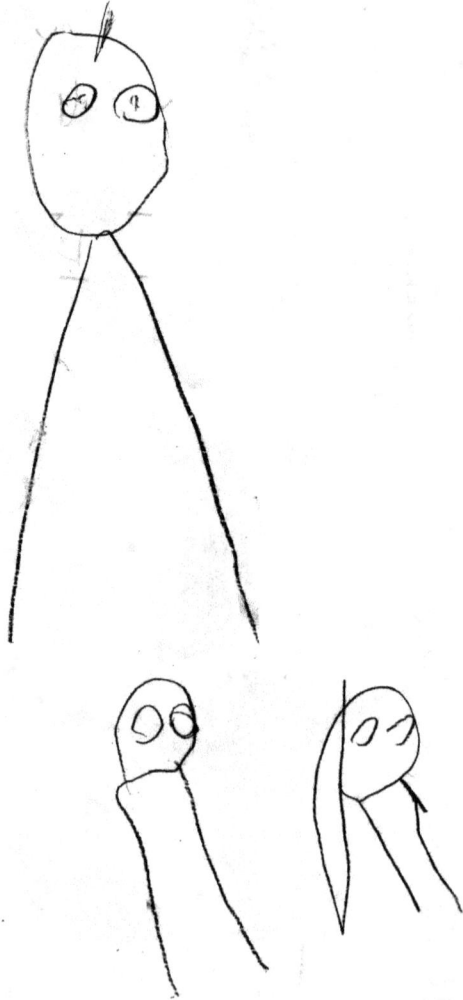

Figure 6: Age 5; Her family.

Figure 7: Age 18; A person of the same sex..

Figure 8: Age 18; A person of the opposite sex.

Figure 9: Age 18; Her family doing something.

Analysis of Tina's Drawings: Exhibitionism – Extreme

Tina's early drawings are bizarre and inconsistent. A drawing of a boy reveals a pair of hauntingly large eyes set in an oddly shaped head, balanced heavily atop spindly, unsteady legs. Another spontaneously drawn boy is notable for pronounced eyes and an appendage between the legs, drawn heavily and aggressively in red, suggesting an enlarged penis. A self-portrait is unbalanced in an opposite way: in her spontaneous drawing of herself, a tiny elongated head with ill-placed facial features sits high on enormously long and uneven legs. This figure simultaneously conveys the grandiose self that Tina presented as a child through the large head and extreme height of the figure, and the unstable nature of her family life and her relationship to the outside world.

In adolescence, Tina's male and female figures are notable for thick, heavy physical forms and multiple transparencies. With exaggerated shoulders, necks and heads atop a faint underlying skeletal structure, the light and wispy facial features are in stark contrast. The faces are strangely withdrawn, with an averted, closed quality. Mouths are open and gaping, yet expressionless, and eyes are half-moons, closed and turned away, the opposite of early drawings which were all eyes, accented aggressively. In these drawings, the line quality of contours of the physical frame and clothing is heavy, while the face and inner frame of the self are faint and unsure.   The physical is brought to the viewer's attention, while the emotional aspect of the self and its identity is avoided, as it is unknowable to the outside, protected from view. Notably, the eyes are closed on both figures, suggesting a preoccupation with the inner world and the fantasy self.

In her family drawing at this age, each figure is separated in space, and appears unrelated to those around it. Each face and head is averted from the other figures, while the bodies appear generic, splayed out and on display. Family members appear clearly separate and on their own, yet simultaneously generic, as though overt roles are defined while the inner self of each is unknown and unimportant. As Tina tended to do in adolescence, this drawing minimizes the importance of both relationships and relatedness in general.

Synopsis

Throughout her first years, Tina was extremely physically active. She loved to run out of the house and down the street with no clothing on in any weather. At such times, she loved being noticed by neighbors and strangers. She came to be highly gratified by being watched—in school, wiggling her backside as she walked; at home, flaunting how she looked in dresses her father had bought her knowing how she liked to show off. He said she was "a little exhibitionist."

Prominent in Tina's attitudes and behavior was a loneliness and a bleakness in her thoughts about relationships and accomplishment. Her interest in clothing, even metal jewelry, was probably related to her earlier exhibitionism as well as to her need for self-protection. Her repeated references to dirt or cleanliness seemed a reverse of her former need to exhibit her body. In fact, her preoccupation with and uneasiness about her body, her athletic ability in tennis, and her diet still reflected her worry about how the world would look upon her. Her interest only in tennis at age eighteen was not strong enough to save her from chronic loneliness or longing for emotional support from some close object; she had developed an almost symbiotic relationship with her mother. In the present, the only hope for someone to fulfill her needs was her brother and her boyfriend.

Subject 4: Will: Cruelty

BO: 1/4
SES: Upper Middle

Will was emotionally neglected from birth; his M was at no time aware of any steps she might take to ease his incessant crying. Early on, he showed intense anger and social withdrawal. His first years were marked by extreme tension and loneliness. Although his intelligence was high, his early childhood was marked by loneliness and disruptive behavior. In following years, his cruelty was expressed in extreme hostility and a marked degree of sadness that he could never articulate.

Confinement Visit with M, Infant age 3 days

M's speech was precise, as if studied, but her manner and gestures led E to feel she was quite anxious. For the first hour, she sat with her hands crossed in her lap, somewhat like a well-behaved girl, friendly but frightened. She was susceptible to periods of depression, she said. She thought discipline should start when a baby began to crawl, and would exert it by taking things away from him, or "a smack on his hands would do the trick," because reasoning would not work for a young child. She thought a baby should not be left alone very much.

Will's visual and auditory responses were normal. He was bottle-fed from the beginning. M had found labor much more painful than expected, although she had been prepared by the LaMaze method. She was "apprehensive" about going home, but was reassured that she would be helped by a nurse for some weeks; otherwise, she said, she would be "very scared" to be on her own with a baby. She was not going to breastfeed him.

Age 6 weeks

After M and Will had been in our office for almost an hour, and Will had cried persistently, M thought he was probably hungry, then rushed his feeding. He fed eagerly, whimpering throughout, with many interruptions when he cried and she picked him up. She attributed his fussing to a "slow nipple," and after each short feeding, replaced him in the crib, though she said he was unhappy when left there. In forty-five minutes he took just three ounces of milk, crying with each interruption. After some time she asked if it would be all right to leave him in the crib even though he would cry; then she continued to have her coffee, evincing no thought about his continuing distress, an early mark of her absence of empathy.

As M had predicted, Will was always unhappy when left in the crib and screamed when food was not immediately given (observed). Usually when M thought he was hungry she gave him his pacifier, but then had to hold it in his mouth, which she found to be "a pain." Also, if the pacifier was removed close to the time of the next feeding, she said that he became angrier. His typical mood was angry; sometimes he cried himself to sleep. There was distance in M's response to him, some annoyance, yet also a quality of pathos; she appeared to feel lost, not knowing how to respond to his unrest, then she spoke with a bit of wry humor of a competition between them as to who would survive whom. She seemed to be substituting a bit of humor for an absence of empathy, still feeling at a loss as to how to help Will to be more comfortable.

Age 6 months

Placed in the crib, Will remained silent and inactive for about thirty minutes except for sometimes staring intensely around the room. Suddenly he turned over rapidly, kicked, crawled about, flailed his arms, and rocked himself. His attention to E was strong, but he lost interest in her as soon as she presented test objects. After a slow initial response to them, his behavior changed radically; all of his movements became fast, excited, and accompanied by rapid breathing. While his attention span to objects was long, his explorative interest in them was moderate. Most of his energy involved transferring and banging the objects rapidly and vigorously, with no facial expression. He did not vocalize at all and never smiled.

M said he liked to be played with in "violent" ways, being

tossed about, hugged, and kissed, but he could play alone for as long as two hours and could sit for long periods quietly, just gazing at things. Or he rocked vigorously and excitedly whenever his diaper was off and played with his feet, hands, and penis. M said she never knew when he was going to be hungry or tired, continually had to readjust her plans, felt very tied down and unable to do even the simplest things like going out of the house, because he was constantly demanding. "I can't count on him for anything," she said sadly. She kept an eye on him as he lay in the crib, ran to his rescue when he got his limbs caught in the slats; but she did not speak to him, nor did he seek solace from her. The absence of communication between them was complete.

Age 1 year

Will's response to all test objects was agile. He peered over the side of the test table to see more of them, went at each with the barest interest, and threw each one away impetuously if he did not at once perceive its explorative possibility. At first it appeared that he did not perceive relationships; soon it became clear that his movements were too rapid for him to carry out most of the tasks. His wish for interaction with E or with action for its own sake was greater than his interest in any test object. He failed to respond to E's demonstrations of tasks that he might perform, although he succeeded in each. Because of his impatience to act, he verged on becoming irritable when an object was placed behind a screen, and showed no joy on refinding it. His most conspicuous activity was to fling both arms upward from time to time (a common gesture of older infants who are asking M to pick them up). Will's M did pick him up, but only to put him on the floor. I surmise that Will's gesture represented his vain wish to be taken up in his M's arms, which she seldom did. On waking from naps he was always extremely irritable; many times she mentioned that he could be alone, but sometimes was so cranky that she had to go to him—then she gave him a bottle of milk or juice and put him back in the crib. She appeared to have no idea of how to respond to him other than mechanically.

He was neither expansive nor withdrawn, always showed interest in M and E, and during testing was negative only when he quickly tired of objects. On his own, he played in a small space on the floor; once on his feet he pulled toys down from shelves, did nothing with them, and then left them on the floor. His vocalizations had an imperious quality, and he appeared to greatly enjoy uttering long, drawn-out vowel sounds repeatedly. This unusual vocalizing might have signified a longing for M's touch or voice. He liked being held more than most year-olds do. He stood alone very briefly but did not seem to enjoy it; M said he could walk on his own (not observed). There were no subtleties in his behavior, such as coyness, sulking, frowning, or even fleeting smiles. Sometimes he clambered onto M's lap with her help, then had to go down again, and so went back and forth many times until she put him in the crib. When he was uncomfortable there, she let him roam around the room. He wandered toward E, who had to keep removing potentially dangerous objects from his path. At the end of the visit when M had to leave the room for a moment he made no sign of noticing her leave, but when she returned he stretched his arms out to her. She said discipline was necessary when he turned on the television, went near the stove, or tore papers. She had to say "No" or sometimes hit his hands. Afterward he "experimented" by touching exactly what he had just been told not to. In other people's homes, she said, he quickly pulled open drawers that in his own home were shut tight. He liked to watch children play, but tried to pull their hair.

M was pleasant and mildly endearing toward Will, expressing neither approval nor disapproval of his behavior, except for slight annoyance when he resisted being dressed. It was as if he was an extra person in the room that she had brought for us to see, and her involvement was minimal, as little as necessary. Only when she was asked what she especially enjoyed about him did she become even mildly effusive, saying she loved to kiss him, especially on his stomach, and loved to watch him play, for then she could sit back and do nothing; and when he was sleeping she loved to watch him because he looked so sweet.

There were some things she wished she had known more about, for example, whether or not to hold him when he wouldn't go to sleep. She had rocked him for a while; then when he was eight months old she let him cry for two nights until he stopped. She also didn't know what to do about "this feeding business." She thought he just lost interest in food.

Age 3 years

(Will was not seen again until age 3. He was one of the last subjects in the first part of this study and was seen only once between ages 1 and 4.)

Will, pale and delicate, maintained a sober expression throughout the visit. Confronted with difficult items, he fretted and whined. Encouraged to try a task on his own, he gritted his teeth and burst into tears, something he did repeatedly when asked to look at or not look at a test object, which made it necessary for E to carry out the test quite gently. His involvement in test tasks was mechanical and poor; he refused all gross motor items. M reported that he adored his bottle. When he was little he didn't drink much until about nine or ten months, when he could hold the bottle by himself. He wanted it so much that recently she did not permit him to take it outdoors. She discouraged its use in the daytime, but he had to have it in order to take a nap or go to sleep, demanded it upon waking in the morning and sometimes awoke in the middle of the night asking for it again. Toilet training had begun a few months ago and was very slow. At first he refused to sit on the toilet, now he could sit there for a long time to no effect. When he didn't want to do something "he was like a stone wall." He was not yet trained at night. In the daytime M let him go about in his underpants, but then he "got nutty" or wild.

She thought of him as being a loner. He liked the idea of playing with other children, but sometimes got over-excited with them. In response to restrictions he became very frustrated and angry, and "tears poured out." A few months ago he began to whine a great deal, which M said drove her crazy, so she tried to be very nice to him, but still sometimes yelled at him. He had many fears, even of his father and uncle. Once he was afraid of going into a grocery store, and cried when M took him in. A few months ago he was afraid of the subway and of watching a television program. He was "sensitive to anything in the atmosphere." At 21 months, when his brother Lewis was born, Will's strongest reaction was to the disruption of his schedule. Soon he was screaming at Lewis to go away, hitting him, or calling M to take him away. E had the impression that in his rapid activity Will was more interested in getting one object after another from E than in the objects themselves. He talked clearly with only slight articulation problems, at first cautiously and slowly, then he appeared to use speech as a means of control. While M referred to Will as being nervous, she kept smoking cigarettes.

F's reports were sparse. He realized that giving Will a bottle in order to sleep was for the parents' convenience, and expressed a belief in treating situations "with reason, rather than specific rules." He thought Will was all right about accepting punishment if he did something wrong, as when recently after he bit Lewis's finger F deprived him of his usual four daily gifts. When he did something that he had been forbidden to do, F might "give him a whack." He thought Will had a "normal lack of confidence," and had seen Will have "what one might call a tantrum" just once, to which F reacted with amusement. Will's greatest fault, he thought, was to be too easy-going. E had the impression that F was given to indulging Will, yet rigid in his expressed belief that parents should follow their own inclinations and not overly sacrifice for their children.

Age 4 years

Will moved into the new situation suspiciously. While engaged in tests he spoke in long, elaborate sentences, so rapidly that he was often difficult to understand; sometimes he engaged in silly-talk or mumbled incomprehensibly, and was unable to relax and enjoy any of the test material. Asked to carry out gross motor tasks, he became tense, almost burst into tears, tried to change the subject by introducing an entirely new one, was unable to say he did not know an answer, or made up one that he obviously knew was not correct. A few months ago he had been enrolled in nursery school but did not like being there "because there were too many children." He cried a great deal when M had to leave and did nothing, so his parents withdrew him. His estimated IQ on the Stanford-Binet was 164.

He ate very little, sometimes nothing at all, preferring meat, pickles, or crackers, and wanted to leave the table as soon as possible. M never pushed food on him; but if he did not eat, she asked him to leave the table. He said he would throw his bottle away on his next birthday; M was not convinced he would. He was always happy to go to bed, as he looked forward to getting his bottle again. Although M had said toilet training began at three years, she now said it started about a month ago. For the first few days, "He wet endlessly—he just didn't want to sit on the toilet," or he would sit there and do nothing. Now he was "pretty good" at urinating in the toilet though still not trained at night. Instead of having a bowel movement on the toilet, he asked for a diaper. M thought he was afraid of the toilet, because he would first say to her "I'll turn my back while you flush the toilet." At home, he wanted M to stay with him all of the time; after using the toilet, he wanted her to wipe him. As usual, she accommodated to his demands. He had "accidents" now and then, when playing outdoors or when excited.

He was angered by restrictions often to the point of crying. He had had many tantrums in his life. When one occurred, M "could not get through to him," so he would just cry and cry. "He's got things going on inside of him, and no one is ever really going to know what they are." M made several references to his "sad inner self," which suggested that she was vaguely aware of his need for comfort. When he cried he often said to her, "Well okay, but dry my tears first." At times, when he was losing control, flailing his arms and legs, she said he was merely being over-exuberant. If his behavior was uncontrollable while visiting another child, she took him home and put him to bed, facilitating his passivity, or she took his toys away and spanked him. She blamed herself for having given in too quickly the past few months when he cried bitterly. She thought that his recent fear of the dark was triggered by his injuring his brother, Lewis, with whom he was extremely rivalrous. Another time, when he hit Lewis so that Lewis fell and broke his arm, Will said, "He knocked the table over on himself." His parents accepted this statement without any discussion, as in similar past instances of his aggression. M found him hard to handle, and said a few months ago she had once thought that he might need psychological help.

F reported that Will gave up his bottle recently, never asked for it again, and now was fully toilet trained. He said almost proudly that Will "was the only nursery school drop out—for some curious reason, he just couldn't stand school," so his parents withdrew him. Asked how Will was with other children, F answered, "He batters people," explaining that Will destroyed things, ran up and down hallways, and spent much time playing alone. At the playground, he was likely to chase other children off a piece of equipment; at home, he tried to find out how things worked, destroying them in the process. Sometimes he broke things "just because he felt like it." F could not explain what Will really liked best to do, because his activities were so "jumpy." He thought Will had nervous mannerisms, probably picked up from F himself. F said that in the supermarket, Will "went insane." Asked what kind of discipline worked best, he said, "Nothing. You have to leave. He won't listen to reason." About Will's tantrums, he said, "They just have to run their course." F said he was lenient, explaining that it took too much effort for him to impose his will, and he was never sure he was right. As to helping Will to do the right thing, he said, "I sort of respect his way of doing things." He liked to think of Will as courageous, which amused M.

Age 5 years

On arrival, Will was fearful and inhibited, hid behind M, entered reluctantly, soon engaged in much masturbatory behavior, refused to look at or speak to E, and stayed very close to M. While they waited for the filming of the M-C play to begin, he cuddled up next to M on the couch, placing his head on her lap and clutching her tightly. Once testing began, he became excited, even euphoric. He carried out simple tasks rapidly, at times deriding their simplicity; he persevered at more difficult ones and succeeded in them with genuine pleasure and pride. His vocabulary was extraordinarily rich, his sentences long and elaborate, his grammar precise. His interest in E pertained only to her role as a tester, although he seemed eager to elicit her recognition of his intellectual ability. He repeatedly made boastful comments about his performance, such as "Too easy," or "This is even easier than the others," or "I keep it a secret from my mother that I'm smart. She thinks she's smarter than me, but she's not." There was no sign that his parents tried to help him develop a sense of reality.

His general mood during his stay was pleasant, but there were signs of uneasiness: he did not engage in tasks demanding the use of both hands; he bit, sucked and chewed on his fingers, pinched his cheeks, pulled at his chin, tugged at his clothing, mouthed test materials, rubbed his arms against the table top, or rubbed his buttocks back and forth on his chair. In response to E's questions he assured her that he did not have to go to the bathroom, then fabricated excuses to explain his inability to respond to some difficult items correctly; for example, "I'm afraid I can't answer that. It would take too long to think about it," or "I can't look at it too closely because my eyes are blinking."

On the WPPSI Will achieved a Verbal IQ of 149 but a Performance IQ of only 115; full-scale IQ, 136. He refused no test items, but was quick to deride the simplistic nature of some questions. Even as he was having some difficulty with his boots, he boasted, "I know everything about which is left and which is right."

On the first days of school, Will stayed for only an hour, demanding that M stay with him. When after two weeks she did not, he screamed, got rigid, and became so upset that the Ts were worried. He stopped crying only after about two hours when the director took him into her office. For many weeks he refused food, could not enter into group activities, and often objected to going to school, complaining of illness or pain. Recently M had wanted to keep him at home because she thought he was ill, but then he cried hysterically, saying it was his turn at school to open the juice bottle. His appetite was still poor. The two children rarely had dinner with their parents, no more than three times a month. (M found that she had "a whole new world" now that both boys were away in the afternoon, and said she thoroughly enjoyed it.)

In the first few weeks of school, he came home wet every day, explaining that he did not like to go to the bathroom there; now it happened almost once a week. Night dryness was achieved a little after age three and a half. During the last year he sometimes asked M to inspect his backside after a bowel movement. He still asked for a nightlight and had difficulty falling asleep, because "bad thoughts" kept him awake; he was evasive about what they were. He dawdled so much that by 7:30 PM M "had had it" and his parents wanted to get their dinner. Each night, he got up for juice that M left for him. In the morning he loved to build "contraptions" using odd pieces of toys, or loved to run wild. In his imaginative play, all the roles he chose were very strong and capable. During the day he liked to draw, write, look at books, or watch television three to four hours a day, and could watch endlessly if left to himself. In the past year he had become interested in rocket ships, animals, airplanes, knights in armor, and undersea life. He wished to excel in everything. Now and then his plans were too grandiose and he became hysterical over small obstacles, yet he refused to accept M's help. Sometimes he was very shy with children, sometimes aggressive. She thought he got into difficulties with them because he hit out or fought "just for the fun of fighting," then added that he got overexcited and could not stop himself from being wild until someone got hurt, or other children asked an adult to "make him stop." Run-ins at home occurred when Will hit Lewis or M, or scattered toys all over the apartment. As an example of his non-hostile destructiveness she described his drawing all over the wall with crayons: "He just likes to draw on things he shouldn't and doesn't set out to spoil them." When he became stubborn, she often isolated him on his bed, tried not to scream at him, but could not always control herself. She did not believe spanking was effective except with young children who could not be reasoned with, and felt that it should be done in anger—a parent who spanked coldly was being cruel. He made demands of M to do things for him, such as to dress him, but she insisted that he do it himself. When he knew he had done something wrong, he might cry, or promise never to do it again (M thought insincerely) or he tried to avoid blame. For example, when recently he scratched Lewis's face, he unhesitatingly told her, "There must have been a chicken in here." As usual, she did not question such excuses although she had concern about his conscience. He recently told her that he had won a game at school by cheating. She chided him but felt troubled only about his obsession to win.

F, on the other hand, told of Will's having adjusted to nursery school and of his hope that Will would learn this year to adapt to social situations without "breaking himself up." His appetite was still poor; he snacked a lot, especially on peanut butter. Occasionally he was constipated. F thought M gave him "some medication" (suppositories) so F did not consider it a problem. At night after the two children were tucked in, a record was put on the phonograph, a light was left on, and the door was closed. Will tossed and turned and sometimes talked unintelligibly. About every two months, he awoke with a nightmare then went back to sleep. F did not know how much a child of Will's age should know about sexual matters, or how much Will grasped of the information he was given. He had observed that Will alternated between imaginative play and "manic" activities. Lately when his parents played table games with him, he tried to change the rules when he was losing. Will always wanted to do things his own way, F said, and got into temper tantrums daily—he might throw himself on the floor, turn red, and say, "You're making me mad!" When frustrated he scratched and picked at his body. M was bothered by this more than F, who found Will to be more obedient than M did. F said that he had no basic differences with M about Will's behavior, then added that M tended to worry about Will's mental health. F guardedly expressed his opinion that the family should just "struggle along," but appeared rigid to the point of being strongly opposed to any regulations such as "formal meals." He placed emphasis on freedom of behavior.

Observation in School, Age 5 years

Will was alert, inquisitive, enjoyed exchanging information with other children, but preferred to work alone as in planning a picture, yet was ill at ease and engaged in constant, compulsive, rapid movement of his legs, while his facial expression remained unchanged. At times he was vibrant and open, then pensive and withdrawn. When he finished his drawing, he wandered about the room aimlessly.

Age 6 years

M looked sturdy, but was totally lacking in spark. Her face was impassive, her voice monotonous, and she spoke only when addressed by others. During the M-C play, she sat stiffly in her chair, usually with her hands clenched in her lap, making no suggestions and rarely speaking to Will. As he was not talkative, silence prevailed during much of the activity. Now and then she smiled or laughed briefly in response to something Will did. He then played alone with the schoolhouse, and for no given reason, had the dolls strike each other over and over again.

Will entered the office silently, looking morose. (M had telephoned us to cancel his appointment because of his suffering a 103 degree fever, then called back an hour later to say that his temperature had dropped considerably and she would come with him after all.) He approached each subtest eagerly, did them rapidly with composure, but responded incorrectly to several verbal items that he had answered correctly at age five; readily said "I don't know" when confronted with difficult items; and worked so slowly that he sometimes answered correctly only after the time limit had expired. (At age five, he had defined a donkey as "an animal with four legs that is very stubborn;" now, at age six, he was content to define it as "something like a horse.") He usually spoke only in response to direct questions.

A year ago, he had occasionally deviated from directions, either to prolong tasks or to modify them, now he did only what was asked of him, but was uneasy as he often scratched and picked his nose, shook his legs, chewed on his fingers, pulled at his lips or clothing, scratched his genitals, and rocked in his chair. He rationalized failure; when asked what was missing in one of the Picture Completion subtests, he said, "I can't find anything missing. I guess that's what's tricky. Some don't have anything missing." In comparison with his boastful behavior a year ago, he was not above saying, "This is sort of hard." He listened carefully to E's directions, followed them silently, yet was often supercilious and condescending toward her. (Many of the themes in his CAT stories centered on children being reprimanded by their parents for not showing good manners.) He left at the end of the testing without a word to E.

Will went back and forth to kindergarten on the school bus, at first only hanging back and watching other children, then had periods of "going berserk," shouting a flow of obscenities. Often he did not eat lunch—not a problem in M's view, because "he always ate bread and milk and didn't starve." He was not reluctant to go to school, although one day he had claimed that his foot hurt so he could not walk, was kept at home, and then made a remarkable recovery. A second brother, Seth, had been born a few weeks ago. During his early days, Will seemed kind toward him. A hostile attitude appeared at school where he made reference to babies "with their dirty diapers" – a projection of his own long-delayed toilet training. At school he had wetting incidents several times a week, explaining to M that he didn't like the toilet there. At home, he didn't like to wash his hands and face, resisted his bath, still needed much help to dress, did not care about grooming, but was overly conscious of how his clothes felt.

He was often critical of other children, saying he didn't like them. At home he always insisted on having his own way. He hated to lose games, and so tried to change rules or to cheat. At home he liked to play with what M called "junk"—pieces of paper and other discarded things out of which he made constructions that he incorporated into imaginative play, in which he was strong and rescued people. He watched television for at least an hour and a half each day, more if he was ill. He loved violent programs, which the parents tried to forbid. M felt the television presented a problem because she tended to let him watch too much. He asked questions about "everything imaginable," had a lot of interest in reading and writing and liked to go to the Metropolitan Museum to see the Egyptian collection, which led him to talk about being buried and put into a tomb. He once said that his bed was a coffin.

M now believed that deprivation was the most effective kind of discipline, so when he fought with Lewis over a toy, she put it away or sent Will to bed. She spanked him about once a week because she herself was angry, although she still thought spanking was effective only when a child was very small and could not be reasoned with. He worried about any new experiences, and tried to avoid them by claiming illness or looking unhappy. Defiant when punished, he promised to do again whatever he was being punished for. When he did something he believed was wrong he might say, "I had an accident" or "I forgot," or try to shift the blame from himself. Once in a while he criticized himself harshly, saying that he was "dumb" or couldn't do something. He was afraid to go anywhere alone. Last year he seemed to fear burglars, then M learned that he wanted them to come so that he could rescue the family. Recently, he had put limits on demonstrations of affection, allowing M to kiss him only on Friday, although he could kiss her whenever he pleased. His most treasured possession now was the towel that he carried around with him and took to bed. Although M did not conceal Will's difficult behavior she spoke with so little involvement that she might have been speaking of someone else's child. She asked no questions about him. Rejoining him after the interview, she said, "I'm knocked out. Are you?"

The parents had placed Will in a private school, in view of past problems. F said that when he entered the five-year-old group, M had stayed in the classroom for two days so he was less upset about her leaving than he had been the previous year;

F admitted that Will still had social problems in school and about every three weeks was reluctant to go. M had read a story to Will about the birth process before Seth was born, since then he had repeatedly asked to hear the story of how he himself had been born. He was at first mildly interested in the baby; then ignored him. F felt Will did not really like the baby.

A week ago at school he had run into a ladder, getting a deep gash on his head that required three stitches. F was proud of the fact that he was very brave and did not cry; later Will was proud of the stitches. His frequent statements about being ill and his pride in receiving medical treatments suggested a reverse of sadism into masochistic pleasure.

At the table he was still restless, and tended to have snacks all day. M and F hardly ever ate with the children, and made no issue of Will's poor table manners. Self-sufficient about preparing for bed, it took him about an hour to fall asleep.

At school, Will had trouble with the rule that children were not allowed to go quickly from one activity to another, and became terribly upset by any direct instruction. At home, he was not a "neatness nut," F said. Will asked questions about spelling, letters and words. "He is a language nut." F then described himself as a "book nut" adding proudly that Will now owned between five and six hundred books. Will had asked his F "What is God," and recently, "Do you believe in King Tut?" F asked Will if he was connecting King Tut with God, and Will said, "Yes, they found his tomb." When Will felt frustrated, he "just cracked for a moment." Discipline was now needed mainly in response to Will's getting wild. F lost his own temper perhaps once a month and might give Will "a spank on his bottom," adding that in the past few months Will had achieved enough self-control for his age, and was typically a mixture of "quiet and thoughtful," "active and busy," or "excited and joyful." When frustrated he became angry, his face got red, he yelled, cried, and hit his fist on the palm of his other hand. F thought Will's most characteristic traits were that he talked a lot, was interesting to converse with, and was most mature in being self-reliant and content to play alone. F could not think of any area in which Will showed the least immaturity, and maintained an air of objectivity and dry humor in talking about him, but like M was extremely protective, and probably withheld information about Will's aggressive behavior. At his request I called M to speak about Will's test performance. She rejoined that Will had always done extraordinarily well on tests, but was not social. She and her husband had sometimes considered therapy for him because of his offensive behavior, and asked whether she should do something now, or wait. I temporized on this because F clearly objected to intervention, but said it did sound as if Will would benefit from some help. If she were then willing, I would look into the family situation at the seven-year visit. M accepted this agreeably.

Age 7 years

As Will had foretold to M, he refused to accept any part of the usual test procedures. He said he hated first grade and didn't have to do anything he didn't want to. Although socializing had not been easy for him, M was sure that he liked school very much and looked forward to seeing his friends.

M was startled to notice that Seth (now 18 months old) ate more than Will did. She had done nothing about his poor appetite other than to encourage him to snack between meals on wholesome foods. He took his big towel to bed with him, rarely was without it at home, slept in a sleeping bag on top of his mattress, and habitually got up every night to go to the kitchen for some food or drink. He still needed urging to get dressed for school, and occasionally returned home with wet pants. As M did not consider this important, she only urged him to be more careful. He was hard to get along with and was often "on the verge of hysteria" because of anger and frustration. With other children he liked to give orders, and tended to get carried away by rough play. When teased he became angry, yelled and cried. He teased Lewis verbally, and occasionally he picked on Seth, although more gently. He talked a lot about robbers, police and prisons, and once he told M that he would not marry or have children because they were "too much trouble."

M punished him frequently for disobedience, was especially

annoyed by his "atrocious" manners, and about every two weeks lost her temper and spanked him. His most characteristic mood, she said, was "sort of manic depressive"—either very high (excited) or very low (mad). She thought he was happy at school when he achieved something, and sometimes happy for no reason at all—he became exuberant, moved a lot, laughed, and giggled. She thought he was not often truly sad, although she used to think of him as having "a burden of sadness." Angry when contradicted or interfered with, he would yell, "You're stupid," cry, and might hit; at times he came close to hitting M. Very often, he was explosively angry and at least once a day cranky and difficult to be with. "Sometimes he snapped out of it," other times he behaved worse. M had tried to impose discipline on him. She believed that although he did not take criticism from others, he constantly criticized himself. When he apologized for something he had done, M was not sure that he felt ashamed (although she believed that his extremely angry reactions were somehow involved with shame). She had found that her threats drew Will further and further into "bad behavior." Sometimes his stories about what happened in school differed from the T's account; M thought he believed his own story and did not mean to deceive. She could not think of anything that made him feel guilty or frightened. Perhaps he may have been upset when he accidentally broke Lewis' finger (the next night he demanded a light in his room). She worried about him but could not explain why, and envisioned his turning out to be "a great person" or "a terrific criminal." She did not know whether his tendency to go to extremes could have been avoided, and did not realize that his violence against his brother and other children signified a need for his parents to take charge of his willful behavior. M was acquiescent and friendly but unvaryingly passive, and emotionally remote. At first she replied mostly in monosyllables; after a while she participated more, though with little affect. At times she gave some indication of her anger and impatience with Will, but usually after making any negative comment, she claimed there had been improvement. Her statement about Will possibly becoming a criminal was made seriously. She reported an unsatisfactory consultation with a child psychologist whom she had visited.

F said Will settled into first grade a few months ago and liked school, although when asked, claimed he did not. Again he referred to how courageous Will had been to accept sutures without anesthesia for his injury on the playground a year ago. There were very few foods that Will liked, F said, and the family's eating habits were "unstructured" and conducive to "nibbling throughout the day." Will awoke every night between 4 and 5 AM and went to the kitchen for orange juice. He sometimes wet himself a little on the way to the bathroom. As he had trouble with his shoelaces, his parents bought him shoes with buckles. He still had definite preferences about the fit of clothing, to which his parents always acceded. After school he played outdoors: he rode his bike, ran around, and visited other children's homes—but while there became frustrated and angry. He told his parents that at school he punched children. Will still altered rules, accused others of cheating, yet cheated whenever he wished.

He had no regular household chores but made up his bed if paid ten cents for doing it—a payment his parents made for a time. F believed that Will liked the feeling that he was agile and athletic, and could not say what Will might dislike about himself, although he needed more discipline than before to control his intemperate outbursts. F would remove the object of his anger and give him "one whack" about once every two weeks. Although Will became explosively angry about once a day, mainly when frustrated, F thought Will had "a modest amount of self-control, considering his temperament," and that his most characteristic mood was "interesting and fun." Will, when angry, turned red, burst into tears and flailed out, but "got over it" in a few minutes. F saw Will's conscience as lenient, and felt no concern about his rigid attachment to a towel as he thought Will did not really need it—he just liked the texture of it. He foresaw that Will would always be intolerant of authority and worried more about his ability to handle situations advantageously than about his rebelliousness, which F said he actually admired. He thought Will had needed more structure when he was younger, but did not think he would have been capable of providing it, even if he could do things over again. He responded to my offer of a post-study visit with interest, then expressed some anxiety about getting advice in psychological terminology.

Post-study interview with M and F

Both parents said they had been concerned about Will's behavior for several years yet had always offered rationalizations for it. F listened passively, raised no questions, and appeared to have no idea of how to evaluate Will's behavior. I was frank about the changes in him from a fearful little boy to one who now made an overt show of strength, but did so awkwardly, rudely, and with open hostility. As I said to them, I was not clearly aware that Will felt shame as M had claimed, but I was sadly impressed by the intensity of his anxieties. They asked for a recommendation for therapy or analysis. I explained why my own choice would be analysis; the decision would rest on who might be available as well as time, finances, and where they would be living next year. F several times said that they would long ago have done something about Will's condition but didn't know to whom to turn; M said she had seen a psychologist recommended by her pediatrician, but he had disturbed her because he discussed Will with her in Will's presence and described his behavior in technical terms without giving M any new way to take action, nor had he recommended any treatment. They were surprisingly and extremely grateful for my offers of help. After making some telephone calls to colleagues in the area where they would be living, I would inform them whom they might see to reserve time with in the fall. They left amicably.

Interview, Age 18 years

On a call to Will's home, I was told by M that he was willing to be interviewed, but would refuse any tests. When I called him a few weeks later to make this appointment, he was immediately huffy and said he didn't think he had any time to see me during the week, and couldn't come on Saturday either, because he "might prefer to do something else on that day—and so wouldn't come anyway." Urged on some more grounds, he coldly told me to hold the wire and went away for four or five minutes until he returned to the phone to say, "I'll see you on February the 27th at 11:30 AM." When I had reason to ask him if he might make it at 11, his answer was terse, "I prefer not to."

When we met he said he had gone to a progressive school that he liked very much because it was entirely informal; there was never any work. He didn't want to go to school, but it didn't matter because there was a lot of freedom. The students designed their own projects for the year; the assignment he chose was to photograph his fellow students at theirs. The class had been good (having an excellent teacher who happened to know Will's father). The next teacher, however, "cracked down" on discipline, as did the principal. Will had felt he was ahead of everybody in his class, and with the new regimented and strict program, no longer saw any use in going to school so that after a few weeks he refused to go. He stayed away until sixth grade (the school sent work home for him, the teachers having been told by his parents that he was not well enough to go to school). His parents took him to a psychiatrist, to whom he refused to speak, and he stayed out of school for several more years. Upon his return, he consistently had fights with classmates. A second psychiatrist prescribed an antidepressant, which he refused to take. Still he didn't want to go to school, feeling he was a stranger there. The family then moved to another county where Will and his brothers all disliked the new school. All this time he was feeling bad, he said. When a third psychiatrist prescribed antidepressants, Will and his parents were scared, and he said to himself, "Okay, I'll become normal," then went to high school for the next three years and always did well.

To fill time when not in school, he took saxophone lessons, but "they were no good" because he understood no concept of how what he was learning was related to music. He really wanted a theoretical background for it. It appeared that he was not one to find any instructions acceptable. When not in school he listened to the radio and learned a lot that way. In high school he didn't like European history, because his teacher "was too much of a scholar and didn't make the subject interesting." He was in Advanced Placement class in chemistry, tutored younger students, but never understood any of it (boasting?)—he just memorized enough to pass tests easily. He liked English if the teachers were all right, but not poetry. He disliked a teacher who had developed his own theories, which Will felt were totally absolute. "If you disagreed, he ripped you apart," and followed with examples of the teacher's ignorance. Although his criticisms might have been valid, the tone of his remarks was harsh and arbitrary. On his SATs, he had a 650 in Math, and a 790 in Verbal.

He had applied to six colleges but probably would not want to attend any of them. One was "too preppy," another had "too many jocks." He got into one of them easily and thought very well of another three, but he would never go to a school he hadn't visited, "And there's no use my visiting until I'm accepted." He had no idea of what he might major in or of what he might like to do some day, and thought the question was pretty silly. In the personal information section of the SAT, where the applicant was to write down his aspiration, Will wrote down engineering although he "hadn't the slightest interest in it." He knew he wanted to make a lot of money. Certainly, he didn't want to be an engineer; that would be about the last thing he would want to do.

He readily volunteered that he had "many good friends" to hang out with at sports games and concerts. He played basketball with his friends at a community center but didn't like the coach there. When he was younger, he played Frisbee. He liked to read science fiction and spy stories and books about music, weapons and armor. Asked about the kind of people he liked to be with, he immediately stiffened and said, "I just couldn't go through everything about other people." Some people thought he was very much like his F. Did F have similar problems in school? He said yes. He couldn't say anything about his parents' personality. Relenting a bit, he added, " Well, I suppose my father is the same as my mother. He's nice and we get along well." M was more social. Sometimes, during high school, F would say to him, "Are you holding together?" They always tried to give him advice, never told him anything about sex but occasionally would say, "Would you like to ask some questions?" He would always say no. He had no idea of where his sexual information came from. About M he could say that sometimes she got angry about little things like his not cleaning up, then imposed punishments that were ridiculous, like taking away the television or the car. When he was younger, probably the worst punishment was to be sent to his room, but not allowed to look at television. What did his parents think about him? They thought he was "intelligent, nice, and had turned out well." M would speak about how beautiful her children were, then if something turned out badly, she got all upset and said she was failing her children. These comments about M were given with less hostility than usual.

The family did some things together, but often could not because each wanted to do something else. Asked what they liked to do, he couldn't mention anything in particular; then said reading, listening to music, and going to lectures about society and ethics. He had no good memories of his childhood except when F took him to the zoo or to museums. He disliked being in the school library, where there must be no talking. "It's not that you're disturbing anybody, but you're communicating in their library, and that bothers them." He was also frustrated by the poor quality of television. His friends thought he was opinionated because often when they liked a program he said, "Oh, that's garbage." He knew it was not garbage, and that he was excessive in his negative remarks, then added that he never lost his temper about anything. "It's better strategically to keep calm." He felt that he was intelligent, in good physical condition, exercised regularly, and got along with people. If he didn't like a person, he tried to hide his feelings, but if he was in a bad mood, he might say to whoever approached him, "Get out of my face," so people thought he was "a stuck-up bastard," or that he was obnoxious. About his conscience he could only say that it didn't bother him because he didn't do anything that would bother it. Sometimes he worried about having a great big career, adding that in a way he was glad he hadn't decided on one, as he wished to pursue a broad range of interests. He had felt isolated from friends in the years he didn't go to school. Referring to that absence he several times said, "I just felt bad." It was hard to know whether he included guilt, sadness, shame, or pride in this feeling. He had no wish to change himself in any way, just to have more fun. As to the needs of children, he asked, "Wasn't this a big philosophical question?," became blank, then said "Well, not discipline, maybe love and affection... well, if not love and affection, then what could there be? What is something that could be just perfect, and the child had it. Would he have everything?" He thought children should have the experience of living in a big city, or have a city mentality. Even with fights it was still better to have siblings. What was not good for children? "Too much discipline and punishment."

He wished he had been able to go to school and behave normally, then mentioned having come to our office to take tests, and there being no point in that. Grumblingly, he said that as he always felt hungry, he was glad to have some cookies and something to drink at our office, but didn't want to be asked to do purposeless things. I offered some of the reasons and how much the study meant to many people; he answered nothing. He valued "ethics but not religion." He could express no strongly held beliefs, so I mentioned capital punishment; he was against it, because it just seemed wrong to kill people. He had no interest in politics. He was "against crime," but he couldn't think of any better system than we had. "Even if some things aren't right for the individual, one has to operate within the system. There are special cases though, as when one has to protest against the Nazis." What did he feel would really make people happier? "Oh yeah, everybody to be happy, and everybody to have money and all that—I have no idea." I dropped the subject. As he had said he wanted to know more about music itself, I asked if he had ever thought of learning to play the piano. "Oh no," he said, "I'm not interested in the theory," contradicting his previous statement. He mentioned various popular musicians whom he liked for their spirit, their ideas and ideals—their ideals were "to get a certain spirituality across." At the end of the interview

I asked him to sign the usual release for his information to be used only for educational purposes. He stood as he read it, signed, then said, "I do not agree to have this interview taped," although obviously I had not taped anything. Asked if he would try the Sentence Completion, he looked at it, put it down and said "No. I just don't want to."

Clinical Impression

Although most of the time Will was detached and acted condescendingly, I felt sorry for him, as he seemed incapable of any natural responses. There could be no doubt about his high intelligence, yet it was sad that he could express no intellectual interest, and lacked any focus. His enjoyment of music, of singing at the community center, and the few remarks about the value of siblings suggested to me a strong affect hunger, and a longing for tenderness that he could in no way admit to himself. He seemed to find safety in his saying "No," as if to shunt off any contact that he would have deemed false. At the end he said he didn't think there was anything of special value about the questions I had asked, because they didn't tell much of anything—they were just usual questions. When I explained that it was not my place or my right to ask him more personal things, though there might be many I should like to ask, my words fell on air. Two ideas about him come to mind: One is that his most positive affect seemed to be directed to F; he mentioned F's collecting books, and his interest in armor. (He had mentioned that he wrote engineering on his SAT application just after telling me proudly that F had lunch with an engineer). I had wondered whether he had had a phobia about going to school. It did not seem so. He seemed depressed in childhood and in adolescence; now my impression was rather that he hid profound anxiety. I did not doubt that he was depressed, especially recalling how he often had said he felt bad. He now appeared to cover over the bad feelings with a perverse negativism that might extend to a paranoid rejection of people and of affects, leading him to ferret out all the possible faults of people. He was certainly an obsessional character who could hardly contain his hatred of something he could not name and who had to maintain a rigid front of pseudo-independence. He appeared to be riddled with fright, anger, sadness and loneliness. In early adolescence he had dared to take religion seriously with a kind of love, which had then turned into an intellectual concern for ethics.

I add three items. One is that it was difficult throughout for Will to make eye contact with me. He shifted his gaze the moment our eyes met. A second was that he referred to the teacher he disliked as "full of shit," which I thought was rather out of place in his relation to me. The third item is that when I asked him in the beginning whether he might agree to now take some of the routine tests, he answered coldly, "I don't wish to concentrate on anything during my vacation." His manner was unyieldingly guarded or overbold, stiff, derogating, mocking interview questions, barely loosened from time to time in response to humor, and showing no intellectual or social aspirations except for the vague interest in ethics, in contrast to the bare hostility that suffused almost everything he said. It was most important for Will to declare that he had no needs; this was a direct reversal of his prolonged infantile longing to satisfy physical and emotional needs. He denied that he ever suffered any loss, and seemed to boast that he was in full charge of himself at all times.

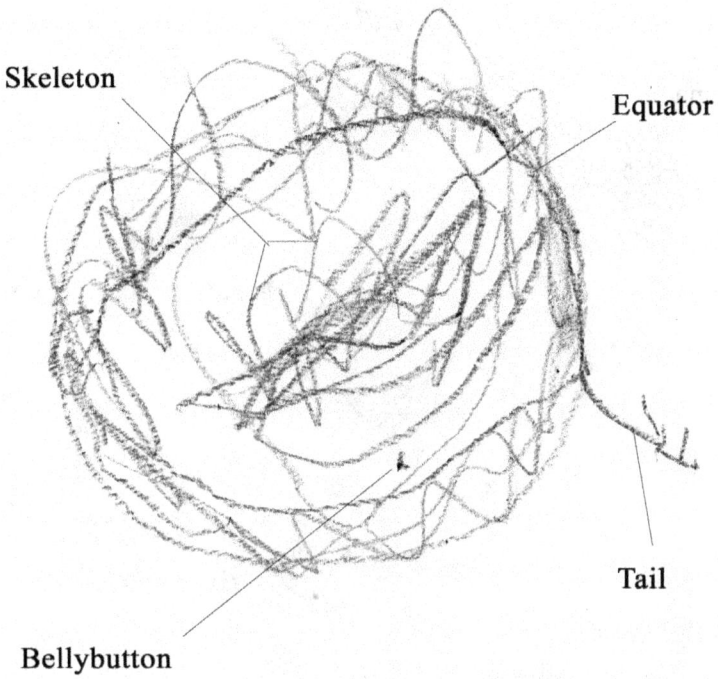

Skeleton

Equator

Tail

Bellybutton

Figure 1: Age 4; A dinosaur.

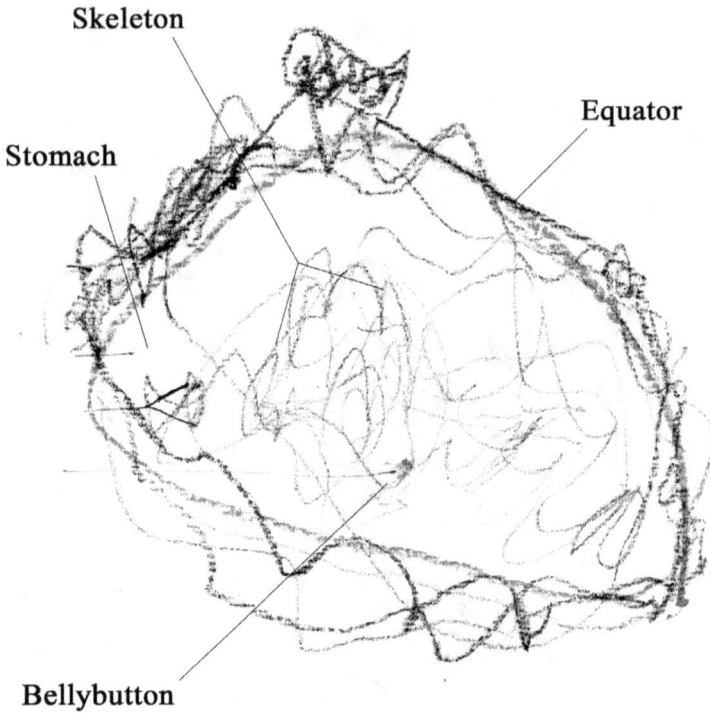

Skeleton

Equator

Stomach

Bellybutton

Figure 2: Age 4; A man.

Figure 3: Age 5; His father.

Figure 4: Age 5; His family.

Analysis of Will's Drawings: Cruelty

Will's earliest drawings at age 4 are unapologetically chaotic, with aggressive scribbling and no discernible form other than a frenetic, cell-like circle. Both a drawing of a man and a spontaneous drawing of a dinosaur appear essentially the same. In his identification of the parts of the drawings, he reveals a superior intellect with which he attempts to compensate for his underdeveloped ability to visually represent forms. When describing both the dinosaur and the man, he points out a "skeleton" and "belly button" in the center of the circle. The whole circular shape is bounded by the "equator." These early drawings demonstrate Will's early lack of interest in complying with the examiner's request, as well as his aggressive, oppositional delight in putting his own idosyncratic markings on the task.

At age 5, Will's drawings are better formed, but retain a sense of chaos, disorganization and self-directedness. Will's father appears in a skewed and marionette-like posture in a spontaneous drawing done in bold, black crayon. Above the figure's head, F's full name appears in big capital letters, followed by F's first name below that and next to the head. Will's own name appears below the figure in even heavier black letters. (In order to keep the subjects anonymous, these names inscribed by Will are omitted from this book.) Four generic figures make up a picture of Will's family, with no gender or size differentiation. All appear to be dancing askew in a posture similar to the portrait of Will's F, with limbs pointing in all four directions. Large heads, wild limbs, and the absence of necks point to a sort of unhinged and unbounded intellectual and physical self. The limbs appear almost broken, a testament to Will's pleasure in his own aggression.

Not surprisingly, Will refused to complete figure drawings at age 18, arguing that the activity was unnecessary and that he did not wish to exert himself. This nonchalant refusal, aggressive in itself, may have represented his attempt to minimize his continued competitive, cruel strivings, and instead to put at the fore both his intellectual capacities and a hint at his vulnerabilities

Synopsis

During Will's infancy and early childhood he was left alone, even when hungry, by M who apparently did not realize how her own history of depression might weaken her capacity to respond naturally to a baby's needs. By about eight months he developed the habit of self-rocking (Brody, 1960); it may have eased his extreme tension and his longing for relief by M. There was no indication that she enjoyed his presence, played with him, or spoke to him; he was often alone even in her presence. In his infancy, she did once say that she loved to look at him when he slept because he looked so sweet.

Will experienced frequent periods of protracted crying until he fell asleep. He took less and less food, and chronically maintained a poor appetite. In his early childhood he probably developed intense anger at M for her incapacity to express any feeling toward him; he was emotionally starved. His behavior as a child was often frantic; it appeared that no comfort was available to him except in the constant carrying of his big towel. The closest he may have come to acknowledging emotional discomfort was in his continuous complaints about the fit of his clothing. His references to "babies, with their dirty diapers" may be understood as a displacement of his own dirty diapers that he maintained until his fifth year; occasionally at age seven, he was still wetting his pants. It is important that when he soiled his underwear his mother sometimes only reminded him to be more careful. There is no further indication that his parents made any effort to help him use the toilet; it appeared that they simply accepted his excuse that he didn't like the school toilets.

During his latency period, increasingly asocial and paranoid ideation occurred. Will was too fearful to socialize with other children toward whom he was either aversive or aggressive. M recognized this; F hardly did. This asocial behavior received little attention from his parents in the same way that his aggressive treatment of his brother escaped their concern. Gradually, his conduct with other children became reckless to the point of cruelty; he always excused it with prevarications. His parents did not take time to reprove him or to explain why his behavior was not socially acceptable; instead they rationalized it. M's usual response to his "wildness" was to put him to bed, which probably encouraged his unconscious passivity. F admired his rebelliousness, which must have promoted Will's identification with F's expressed freedom from anxiety and denial of any need to trust authority.

In adolescence he did not appear to behave with cruelty, but retained hostile attitudes, apparently unable to focus any efforts toward socialization. His negativism brought him to reject the social overtures of other children and to oppose or condemn any adults in positions of authority. In this stance, he stayed out of school for almost six years; his parents only made excuses for his absence. His attitudes of superiority and his wish to control all others (with the possible exception of M) appeared to have been related to hidden feelings of protracted shame of his inability to learn a normal use of the toilet. Possibly related to the conscious or unconscious shame was a hidden fear of ultimate punishment by his parents for the continuous soiling of his underwear.

Subject 5: Gail

BO: 3/5
SES: Middle

Gail showed none of the behaviors reflecting the negative aspects of the component instincts as originally described by Freud. These brief accounts of her in early childhood and at age eighteen are presented to indicate the manifest difference in her behavior from that of the other four subjects who have been described.

Confinement visit with M, Infant age 3 days

M was a woman of medium height in her late thirties, dressed for comfort rather than style. She carried herself erectly, sat comfortably, with a great deal of latent activity expressed in her quietness. After college graduation, she had volunteered at an organization for the homeless. She said briefly that delivery was quick and easy, with no medication and no episiotomy. She described Gail as lively and active, having a vigorous cry, in almost constant motion when awake, and not at all irritable. She reassured SB that she would gladly participate in our program, although there might be some problems with the date of meetings because of her older children.

Gail's visual and auditory reactions were normal as were her head and body movements. She could turn her head and lift it off the bed within a minute. Breastfeeding was entirely satisfactory.

Age 6 weeks

Gail's regard of E had a trance-like quality, as if she could not free herself from it, except for E's effort to direct her attention to test objects. She focused on the red dangling ring for six or seven seconds, then again maintained her gaze at E; she held the rattle firmly, tried to imitate E's shaking it and after a few attempts managed to do so. Although she was not yet nine weeks old, her hands were relaxed and open, and all her movements were remarkably well-integrated. M carried her in a vertical position in a sling held against her chest, or kept her in a carriage to protect her from the older, active siblings. She described Gail as typically either contented or crying, and gurgling happily when tickled.

Age 6 months

Gail's response to all objects was quick. After completing the easier tasks she readily discarded them. Concentration on the more difficult ones was very solid. Her insight into tasks was most readily seen when she was given the ball and the mirror. She not only touched the ball to the mirror easily, but also watched herself doing so and then watched the reflection of the ball and her hand from several angles. Her holding of test objects gradually increased, and while she looked at them in her hand she engaged in wrist-turning, dropping and retrieving them, sometimes banging them.

M said Gail was content to lie quietly for long periods, moving hardly at all although her facial expression was quite alive. She howled when taken from one breast to the other. At other times she grinned, laughed, or was coy; she frowned when left alone but did not cry. Until the end of her feeding she made almost no sounds at all, then suddenly burst into a bubble of vocalizations, nicely modulated, with a good deal of affect. She grinned once or twice, had a big smile, and just once was a bit bashful.

M's reports were sparse; her attitude was loving yet casual.

Age 1 year

Gail was big and hefty. Motor activity occupied her most, perceptual activity less so, and social activity least. When her demands for food were not acceded to readily she became tense, flushed, and screamed; these little tantrums were short-lived. She responded to all test objects eagerly. Her concentration on the more difficult items was sound.

M said that Gail had started to crawl a few weeks ago, now loved it, and also loved to tease by trying with a grin to get at books and records that she knew she was not supposed to touch, taking any chance she could to pull them out. She liked to roughhouse with her brother Ben (age three), and to squeal and roar, imitating F at play with her. When M said "Dada," Gail repeated it and looked around for F. She enjoyed watching M do things in the kitchen, especially if M sang to her while at work. M had heard her express specific consonants: "Day-day" for her sister Dana, "Mama," a word for "hot," and for "thank you." When she wanted to be changed she kicked her legs, or arched her back, or bounced on her bottom. She liked to play with pots and pans and to tear paper; best of all, she loved reciprocal chattering. She was always eager to get at books; usually M could stop her with a sharp "No!"

M was at all times casual and business-like. The only time she stopped for pure fun was when, imitating F, she showed E how she could growl like a lion to make a delighted Gail scramble to her. If F, on coming home passed by her too quickly, she made a lot of noise, demanding that he pay attention to her.

Age 2 years, 6 months

Gail was tall and heavy, with well-developed speech. Her performance of all gross and fine motor tasks was superior; her expressive behavior was greatest vocally. E saw anger, smiling, and irritable crying but no subtle facial expressions except for the way Gail held the ball in her hand to the mirror.

M was casual, reported that Gail played well by herself, with crayons or puzzles, did not seek out jobs but was happy when given one, as when she spied a broom or sponge and had the idea of using it. She had a habit of getting out of bed at night when not sleepy. M found that the easiest way to handle this was pretending not to notice, then Gail went back to her bed.

She preferred quiet activities, loved to listen to records of music or to fairy-tales, could play by herself for at least an hour at a time, and liked to dress and nurse her dolls. Discipline was needed when she did something she was told not to do, for example, when she played with noisy toys early in the morning. She was becoming more responsive to requests made of her, and had begun to grasp the efficacy of compromise. She adored animals and played with the family dog roughly or gently as her mood dictated.

F put the children to bed four or five nights a week. They insisted that M read a story to them every night, then F sang to them, then the children sang, and after that they fell asleep. F said Gail showed tenderness and compassion when anyone in the family was not well, could be generous as well as possessive, and had the courage that went with her independence, which he had observed since she began to talk at age one.

Age 3 years

Gail was robust, animated, and engaging. She immediately began to speak with E, smiling as she responded to E's comments. Her movements were slow but systematic and well coordinated. While she was stringing some wooden beads she said to M, "It's going to be a pretty necklace." M asked if it was for the little teddy bear that Gail was keeping near her. "No," Gail answered, "he's too little. It's for you." M reported that she was beginning to rebel against parental authority, for which she was occasionally deprived of dessert or lightly spanked; M said regretfully that she knew no other way to make Gail mind. On one day when she insisted that Gail eat her egg at breakfast as her siblings did, Gail sat with the egg in her mouth for more than two hours before M gave up.

Age 4 years

Gail's whole face lit up when she smiled. She could organize and complete an activity of her own choice, and was trying to read and write. She liked to dance, to make up songs, and listen to stories. How she reacted to restrictions depended on whether or not she felt they were reasonable; if she felt they were unjust she "raised hell—she fussed, screamed, cried, kicked— and the works," but was eased by being taken onto M's lap and talked to softly, though she had a new habit of whining and complaining. In school she was sober, and able to show a relaxed contentment in social overtures. Her strength appeared to be a certain integrity, an ability to move according to her own wishes yet able to comply with the demands of the group. On the Stanford-Binet her IQ was 129.

F reported that Gail was a light sleeper and often went to her parents' bed during the night. They would tell her to go back to her own bed, which she did, sometimes after ten or fifteen minutes. When alone she played with her dolls, sang to herself, or played with crayons. She participated actively with other children, taking the initiative about half of the time. She had two imaginary friends, and she was especially happy at school, chatting merrily, or listening to records. At home she became unhappy when she felt attention was given to her siblings instead of to her. She reflected an emotional freedom for social and thoughtful activity, for the development of firm object relationships, of play that might form a capacity for sublimation, and of character strength. She was able to show joy, generosity, and sadness.

Age 5 Years

Gail was animated and wholesome looking. Her mouth was forever upturned in a radiant smile. She spoke exceedingly rapidly and had a tendency to run sentences together; when excited her voice was loud and shrill, almost shrieking; yet her speech was distinct, clear and expressive because of her superior vocabulary. She often gesticulated excitedly while speaking. At all times she was cheerful. She ran the gamut of emotional responses, her behavior undergoing gradual but startling change as her confidence in the environment increased. She responded to questions agreeably, always with a smile. This outgoing demeanor was soon replaced by clowning behavior. She clapped her hands and giggled uproariously, making silly noises. Her comments to E became preachy. As items were becoming difficult, she shouted, "No!" or "I don't know," then might tell an exceedingly brief story about the CAT card and quickly state, "That's the end." Thus, when M entered the room and said that it was time to leave she shouted, "No!" When M asked if her stay at the project had been enjoyable, Gail exclaimed "No!" and as they left our office she refused to look at or speak to E. E could not recall a moment when Gail was not either sucking her thumb, chewing on her fingers, sucking on a pencil, scratching or rubbing some part of her body, banging her knees together, tugging on her clothing, fiddling with her hair, clutching her genitals, or scratching her belly. Her responses were quick, as she found most test items easy. During pauses she fidgeted in her chair, kicked her legs, rocked her chair, tilted it back against the wall, alternately stood up and sat down again, and tapped her feet. When asked to draw pictures of her family members, Gail began work at once, holding a pencil comfortably in her right hand, and referred to the personal quality of each person she was drawing. Presented with the Block Sort test she worked quickly, saying, "squares, rounds, triangles." As she went on, she said, "The little ones go together, these are middle-sized... middle-sized and middle-sized. Big, big, big." She then counted all the groups and said, "There are more bigs than little ones," received a perfect score on this subtest, then replaced all the blocks in their containers according to shape.

Gail was inquisitive and had an excellent memory, but impulsiveness appeared to impede her intellectual responses. After overcoming her original shyness, she became silly. This change in her behavior appeared to represent an advance from her good little girl behavior at age four to a show of toughness and sureness, often seen in the movement of a child from age four to age five. At all times it seemed clear that she was aware of behaving inappropriately and wished to demonstrate her capacity to be outspoken and unafraid.

M reported that there were no eating problems and that there had been no essential changes in the bedtime routine except that F worked late and didn't sing to the children as often. Gail's interests were expanding. She now was concerned with developing skills with numbers and letters. She did not especially like to do any chores, but cleared the table and washed dishes a few times. She was sensitive to others' feelings and very aware of what it meant to be hurt; when a favorite toy was broken, she became rather melodramatically upset and shed tears. She was angered by what was to her mind unfair treatment, and showed it by crying or stamping her foot. When feeling hurt or disappointed, she ran off alone, cried, and sucked her thumb. A good way to get her into a better mood was to ask her to join in an activity. She was embarrassed about her thumb sucking but could not stop it, was generally obedient, and stubborn only if she felt that she was being imposed upon, such as when an assigned task seemed too difficult. Discipline might be necessary when she had differences with her siblings; in such cases M separated them and made Gail sit in a chair for a time. She considered Gail to be neither too submissive nor too aggressive with children, did not know whether she might be a leader, but felt sure that she would not be "an abject follower." When she felt or knew she had done something wrong, she cried and was sorry, but would willfully go against M's orders if she did not accept them. She had a strong conscience, was not strict toward the faults of other children if they were insignificant, but could make a big issue of misdeeds she considered wrong. M thought the root of this problem was her position in the center of the family and believed Gail deserved more attention than she got. As usual, M was friendly and at ease with all the project staff, although she was obviously tired. She was never inattentive, and at the end spoke of her enjoyment of our sessions. Her reports were at all times full, articulate, and relevant.

Observation in School: Age 5 years, 4 months

Gail did not realize she was the focus of O's attention, occasionally looked at her with mild curiosity, but just as readily turned to another child to tell him a story and made no further attempts to figure out who O was or what she was doing in the classroom. Strengths noted were her enjoyment of skills, ability to work alone, interest in learning, and flexibility. Her eyes grew large with excitement as she worked with an assistant teacher and other children. When T asked for spontaneous contributions, Gail was always the first to think of a word. For the letter V there was initial silence from all of the children. Gail smiled, and came out with "victory" and "volcano." She showed ability and desire to succeed physically as well as mentally. During indoor play she won the girls' race from one end of the gym to the other, then won the runoff between herself and the winner of the boys' race. Soon, she skipped with two of her friends following her to the far end of the room to watch some block building there. After a quick glance at the "castle" she fell to the floor as though an arrow had struck her. Her two friends toppled down too, in imitation. Soon they were all rebuilding the castle. Later she climbed up slowly on a little table and on her knees, looked over the shoulder of a boy reading a book without disturbing him, and then picked up the book and began to read it to herself. The teacher asked her to read it aloud to the class, and she sat in her chair with all the other children in a circle around her; poised, with her whole effort directed toward getting the story across in an interesting way. She showed the pictures to the class at appropriate times and read at a tempo that was challenging. A few times, she spontaneously hugged her constant girl companion for the day and vice versa.

Age 6 Years

Gail was dressed neatly, and wore a long gold chain that she fiddled with throughout the session. She had a sophisticated vocabulary, spoke in full sentences and generally made no grammatical errors. Her movements were smooth, sometimes a little slow, perhaps reflecting her desire to think things through before expressing herself. During the M-C play their interaction was altogether amicable. At times there appeared to be a bit of tension between them, as when in a sing-song voice Gail said, "Mom, you've done it wrong. It's supposed to go like that." A possible conflict of wills occurred when Gail did not wish to place a male doll in the schoolhouse. (O believed it was at the prodding of M that Gail had identified the doll as Daddy). Gail then threw the doll back in the box saying, "Daddy's at work."

During the administration of the WISC subtests her perseverance was exceptional. She smiled often, was willing to try tasks that were difficult, enjoying the intellectual challenge. When E once suggested that she make a guess at an answer, Gail said, "I'll think that over." There was a pause as she thought and then did respond. She studied all the pictures for quite some time, then arranged them in the correct order. She answered almost every vocabulary item with a full sentence, incorporating the question into her answer. She also carried over one Verbal subtest into the next. For example, when asked to explain how pairs of items were alike, and later to define a series of words, she began the task of defining the series of words by first showing how they were similar or dissimilar to each other and then defining them. A great amount of physical activity contrasted with her otherwise mature and sophisticated behavior. She had a long attention span and an extremely well developed ability to stick to a task.

Gail entered a new school and within two weeks was able to walk to school alone. Her usual bedtime procedures had changed in that her older sister or brother now read the nightly story to her, then F said a prayer with the children. Gail was slow about getting to bed, as she dawdled "by nature" which made M impatient enough to give Gail a "spank." If she napped during the day, she had trouble falling asleep, so her parents let her come into the living room and talk with them a while. Once asleep she slept soundly. She managed toilet routines on her own, though sometimes M might have to remind her to wipe, flush, and wash her hands. M usually chose what Gail was to wear, but if Gail had a strong dislike of a garment she was adamant in her refusal to wear it. She was beginning to prefer to be with her friends more than with her family. She interceded when any of her siblings got into trouble, tried to be a peacemaker, and often had a wise comment to make to them. M found that Gail was able to see interesting and sophisticated relationships within a situation.

Rather than being critical of other children Gail was sensitive to their feelings. She liked to take the lead but did not often insist on having her own way. When she was teased, she cried a little and hit. She took losing fairly well, but when playing with her siblings, she sometimes accused them of cheating. Her play was basically quiet. She was self-sufficient but could accept help when needed, and sometimes had to be urged to tidy up; M often found it was not worthwhile to force her, although she tried to as a matter of principle. Gail often said, "I want to help, but I just can't." Gail had watched little television in recent months, on and off for about two hours a day. M forbade violent shows. Sometimes Gail spoke of heaven and of relatives that might be there, and said, "This happened because God wanted it." M found her most difficult behavior to be her refusal to help with picking up at home (she was cooperative at school). Asked how often she found it necessary to give Gail a spank, she replied, "Once every thirty-six hours." If Gail saw a distressed person or animal, in real situations or on television, she brooded over it for a while. When criticized, she became quiet or cried, depending on the severity of the criticism. She accepted punishment if she thought it was justified; otherwise she complained loudly. Nearly constant thumb sucking continued. With Gail's cooperation M had tried using bad tasting medicine on her thumb to no effect. Now the parents were trying to work through her vanity by stressing that she would ruin her teeth.

M was compliant in her responses but made no attempt to stifle her frequent yawning.

F said Gail now shared her room with her older sister Dana, was self-sufficient about preparing for bed, and liked to read in bed as her sister did. In the morning she needed urging to dress but no help in dressing, though she moved slowly. F said she had a low threshold of tolerance for teasing that was meant to hurt, and reacted with tears, but if she was teased jokingly she took it with humor. When she won games in play with other children, she never boasted, "but smiled all over." She was very eager to learn math and wanted to imitate her brother especially, as he was an excellent scholar. F commented that her interest in her Barbie doll was mature in its indication of curiosity about adult female anatomy. Household routines bored her but she was very good at fulfilling school tasks and writing birthday notes and thank you letters. Recently she had needed more discipline because she had become so assertive, and the best way to handle her was to speak softly to her. F felt that Gail had not achieved enough self-control for a child her age because she cried too readily, and became angry when she could not get the attention she needed, marching off in a huff or crying. The only situation that he could think of that had made her sad was when her little sister Betsy was hurt and needed to have a stitch. Gail had cried along with her. He saw her most conspicuous traits as her excellent sense of humor ("She is a good punster"), her interest in learning and schoolwork, her ability to play contentedly alone, and her capacity to be pleasant, outgoing, and collaborative. She showed most maturity in her ability to accept her parents' direction and her own or her siblings' limitations, while her tendency to withdraw from a troubling situation demonstrated less maturity. F's manner was relaxed, friendly and humorous. His reports were brief, not particularly perceptive, but he had warmth, true involvement in his paternal role, and conveyed an attitude of great interest in and appreciation of our work.

Age 7 years

Gail looked sturdy. She had a crumpled "after school" look but was clean. She said that she had been working with clay at school all day, as was evidenced by her hands. Her speech was well developed; she tended to be talkative, cooperative, and alert, rarely let an item pass until she tried to answer it, and answered in full sentences with few grammatical errors. On some of the subtests she might have received more credit if she had worked with more speed.

On the WRAT* her reading score was equivalent to a grade of 4.1, her spelling to a grade of 3.7 and her arithmetic score to a grade of 2.4. The thing she liked best about school was "You learn a lot. Some schools give recess like ours, you get gym, and sometimes you get parties and food to eat." The most pleasant thing she could think of was "Nature...I really do like all sorts of animals, trees, and grass." What she liked least about school was "by the time you're home, you're so tired." Toward E she was courteous, friendly, and ready to respond appropriately, appearing to be thoughtful and level-headed. Her intellectual

* See index.

abilities were superior and her aspirations high. She handled all social interactions with poise. The only detraction from her social contacts appeared to be her tendency to talk over and beyond the topic at hand.

M said she liked going to school. Although usually slow-moving, she was the first one out in the morning. Gail dressed herself except for a possible zipper or button in the back. She loved to watch television, swim, and play with her dolls, but if she had her choice of swimming or television she would prefer swimming. Rock collecting was her new hobby. She had been trying to match them to pictures in a book that she had about rocks. Just yesterday she mentioned that she would like to be a geologist. She had a doll collection that was more for looking at than playing with. Her regular household chore was to make her own bed, and sometimes she might walk the dog. M had a rotating system of breakfast, lunch, and dinner table setting. Gail resisted her turn. She might get a little money for doing a job, but would rather not do the job. M noted that Gail was reflective, could grasp underlying meanings, and that a great deal went on in her mind that she didn't express. She needed no prompting about homework, was "a nut" about getting places on time, but was not good about keeping track of her possessions or managing her school notebook. She could be self-centered and forgetful. "She is not rebellious yet," said M, "but is slowly getting there." With regard to frustrations or disappointments, she reacted with weeping and wailing. This did not occur often, but when it did, "she really goes at it." She was an "independent soul." M thought Gail liked about herself that she had dignity and self-respect, had been admiring herself for a long time, and was determined to keep her nice figure.

M described Gail as pleasant, calm, good-natured, reserved, and introspective, becoming terribly upset only if she saw someone else's feelings being hurt, and reacting to any punishment as a "gross injustice." She wished that Gail had better control of her speech, noting that there was so much talk among all the children that Gail had to struggle to get the floor, yet when she talked, she took in all possibilities, taking five minutes to say what another child would say in one. M noted that Gail was lethargic even in the womb, and as a baby was always undemanding, and happy to observe instead of participating. She regretted not having enough time to give to her children, so that the potential of each was not fully developed and seemed to experience the trip to the city for this interview as something of a holiday, a respite from her bustling home where she needed more time to rest.

Tests, Age 18 Years

Gail was tall and stocky. She easily made eye contact and when relaxed had a particularly pleasant smile. She was ready to take on the challenge presented by the tasks, and worked to completion, after which she relaxed, smiled, and was animated. She had a normal degree of anxiety during the administration of the Rorschach. Despite the high level of her intellectual potential and achievement, she experienced herself as physically damaged and emotionally vulnerable. She maintained a heavy reliance on intellectualization; at times it led her to strive for more than she could comfortably do and made her appear pedantic. Overall, she was functioning at a very superior intellectual level. On the WAIS-R, she achieved a full scale IQ of 138, highlighting the fact that she was an overachiever in verbal areas, probably due to social maturity. Her strengths lay in her ability to attend and her excellent practical judgment. She was overly concerned about conforming and had a tendency to be self-deprecating, expressed in a degree of emotional constriction. Although having the ability to be emotionally related to others and socially active, she was more comfortable if her social contacts were made on her own terms, as occasionally she needed to keep distance in order to protect herself from criticism she anticipated. Her anxiety increased when she was presented with masculine images. She experienced M as unempathic, controlling, and at times intrusive, viewing F more benignly, though she felt he treated her like a little girl. The nature of the familial tension was not clear, nor was it clear whether she felt they shut her out or she had opted out, but as she was still only seventeen her tensions about herself were not unusual. She strove successfully for independent functioning and was flexible in her need to ask for help, though she tended to deny her need for emotional support.

Diagnostic Statement[19]

No psychological diagnosis. Obsessive-compulsive and narcissistic traits.

Interview, Age 18 years

Arrangements for this interview were made easily. Gail gave much information in an organized way.

School always went easily and well, except when an eye problem had occurred in the second grade. She had astigmatism and strabismus, had to wear a patch and glasses, was teased by the classmates because of it, and felt unaccepted. In Junior High she became very involved in learning, in drama groups, and in clubs devoted to language and other cultures. In tenth grade she chose Latin, was the youngest student in her class, received an 85 on a third year Regents, and was at the top of her class. She spoke often of how much she loved learning. In eleventh grade she worked at a school for retarded children, and in a home for blind, aged people. Her SAT scores were a total of 1280, with the math score about 30 points higher than the English. She also worked with the soccer teachers at a recreational center where she cared for children between ages five and twelve, at the City Realty Board, and as a volunteer at the town library. She ranked 34 out of 725 students, with an average of 94.8.

She applied to several first-rate colleges and was happily accepted to one in the Midwest that offered a great deal of much needed financial aid, and a work-study program. She mentioned her love of language and cultures, and her intimate friends. They went to the movies and to each other's houses, and talked about sports and reading. She spoke at length of her interest in poetry, research papers, music, literature, and

---

[19]D.S. always made by the psychologist who administered the tests.

historical works, noting her penchant for the humanities rather than the sciences.

Gail's parents had little time or money to go out much and mostly stayed at home and read. M was hard working, did community work, gardened, and liked to cook. She was a real friend, although they had occasional spats. F's interest was in coaching, the community, and being involved with his family, for all of whom he felt deeply. When the children were younger they did many things with the parents. Her sister Dana was less of a student than Gail, but was a very caring person. Ben was the most well-disciplined person Gail knew. She admired him so much because in the ninth or tenth grade he lost interest in school and wanted only to be with his friends, but then pulled himself together and knew what he really wanted to do. Their youngest sister Betsy was the psychologist in the family and had the best relationships with all of its members. There were many little fights, but in the end they all compromised and were close. Gail had never needed discipline at all, or what had been administered was just right. In the third or fourth grade, as she remembered, when the children disobeyed they had to write something out like: "I will not—." That penalty did not work out, so M made the punishment fit the crime: if the crime was a big one, she chose a long piece of writing for the culprit to copy, such as "Hiawatha," though the version that she chose was really a spoof on the poem, giving the children much to laugh at. The point was that M did not force them to do something they disliked, but gave them a constructive punishment to make up for something they had done that was not constructive. Gail remembered having had to write reports on Abraham Lincoln. It appeared that M invoked a punishment that was not derogatory.

Gail was irritated by unnecessary meanness or ridicule; she remembered being the victim of ridicule because of her eye patch in the second and third grades. Then she got angry and lashed back at people. When Ben and Dana laughed at her or spoke sharply to her, she lost her temper and would go at them briefly with words, but never blows. She was also angry when she saw people not caring for others, even in fiction. She didn't like to tell M when her older sister and brother bothered her, or how it hurt her when they thought of her as a "funny little twerp." Anyone with a good sense of humor made her feel good, as did "knowing I did something good for someone or for myself. I'm basically happy if I do something purposeful." Her parents would say she didn't have a mean streak in her, but she could be angry and nasty. Her conscience was very strong; for example, though she had no need of the credits for a physics test she had taken a few days before, she still felt she should have studied more for it. When asked what might have troubled her in her growing up, she said, "You mean beside my eyes?" Then she spoke of the great difficulty of managing her hair, and of her worry about not being thinner. She was troubled by her thumb-sucking, which had continued until second grade, when one day she just decided she had to stop. She had no fear of dying because she truly believed in something like ghosts who would return to life, and was not afraid of oblivion. She wished she could be more decisive. "In this world you have to know where you're going. You have to... study to equip yourself for a profession."

She would like three children. One would be too alone, and two are not bad; she would just rather have three. Children need somebody around to care for them, love them, and help understand their needs. Children have so much to learn in their early years, when their personality is molded. At least one parent should be around them all the time. Gail wouldn't want to work for at least five years after her baby was born. Adolescents need understanding and patience, and lots of discipline, because they test you so much to see what you are going to do or give them. There shouldn't be any pussy-footing around on either the adolescents' or the parents' side. She would like her children to have experiences with different kinds of people and places so that when they were older they would have open minds. In all honesty she could not think of any way she would like to relive her life differently.

She spoke at length about her values regarding marriage ("for keeps"), living with sisters and brothers, and having to attend to your body as well as your mind. If she had a daughter, she would not encourage daintiness in her; femininity, yes, but not just being pretty. Her strongest belief was about abortion: "If the unwanted child turns out to be psychologically or physically deformed, that could ruin both lives. Abortion is like euthanasia in a positive sense." About murder she thought that only if the guilt was absolutely clear would she say yes to corporal punishment.

If she could serve as an example for just one person, she would feel she had a worthwhile life. She took a couple of minutes to think of someone whom she distinctly admired before she said Golda Meier, because she had a dream and accomplished what she wanted to. She admired her parents greatly because they had given a great deal to the children, even though they didn't think so.

Clinical impression:

Gail was a very big girl, weighing about 150 pounds and was about 5'6" in height. The bigness came not only from her size, but from her large round face, and a great deal of very curly hair. She spoke, moved, and walked with strength, and made her presence felt dynamically. She brimmed with mental energy, but physically was altogether quiet and composed. Her comments suggested an unwavering aim to be a solid citizen and to be productive for herself and others. It was clear that she had many friends of both sexes at school, but that her strongest attachments were to family members.

Some anxiety lurked in her reported fear of ghosts. It appeared to be a mixture of fear, worry, and real interest. "Even if I didn't believe in an afterlife I would fear death." Her grandmother's death was her first experience of death (when she was eleven) and this belief in ghosts may have hidden a fear of death. Aspects of a wish to be seen and heard appeared to a very moderate degree in her chattiness, which sometimes stretched a little beyond the reasonable expectation of a listener's attention; this might be a remnant of a young child's normal anxiety about how to be noticed. In Gail's case her parents' praise for her older brother's academic achievements may have influenced her tendency to over-express. Her abundant speech and her emphasis on moral and ethical behavior might also suggest a hidden anxiety about impulsivity which, if acted out, would arouse too much inner conflict, but these affects are not unusual for an adolescent. She appeared to be a fine human being with indications of a wholesome future. Possibly she showed an excessive reliance on reaction-formations.

Figure 1: Age 4; A girl.

Figure 2: Age 5; Herself.

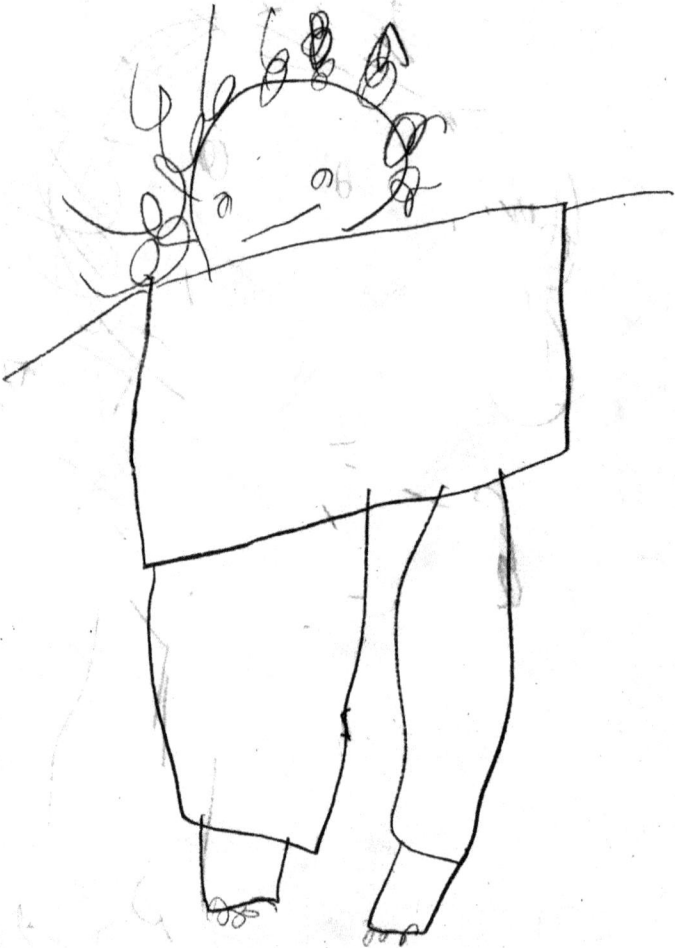

Figure 3: Age 5; Her sister.

Figure 4: Age 5; Another of her sisters.

Figure 5: Age 5; Her brother (holding a butterfly).

Figure 6: Age 5; Her mother.

Figure 7: Age 5; Her father.

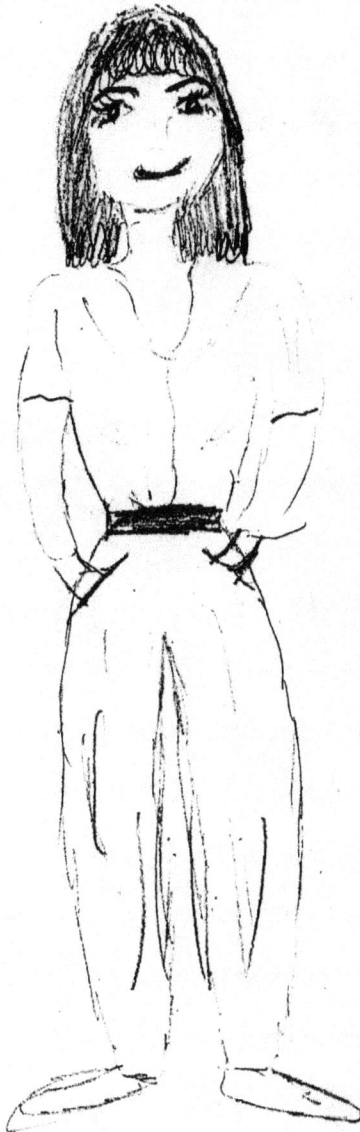

Figure 8: Age 18; A person of the same sex.

Figure 9: Age 18; A person of the opposite sex.

Figure 10: Age 18; Her family doing something.

Analysis of Gail's Drawings: Adaptive Development

Gail's earliest drawing, at age 4, of a girl, is drawn in a relatively balanced and detailed manner. Her forms and line quality are quite strong, in keeping with her precocious attentiveness, ability to organize, and strong cognitive and motor development. A head/body is formed by a completed circle of unwavering line. The features of the face are all included – eyes, nose and mouth – and are strikingly proportional, with a lack of a physical core, not uncommon for children her age. She gives gender appropriate personal detail to the drawing of a girl by adding an odd, asymmetrical crop of hair. Arms and legs are well drawn, with steady lines, although the hands are striking in their large, sharp forms, perhaps indicating Gail's noted impulsivity combined with her quick and competent grasp of objects in her environment and her strong wish to seek out and explore her surroundings.

Again, at age 5, Gail seems to take great enjoyment in describing her family in multiple, detailed drawings. While her figures show some mild asymmetry and inconsistent inclusion of hands, they are generally sturdy, with well-defined facial features, arms and legs. As described in her early preschool years, Gail seeks out people, is sensitive to their emotions, views them as individuals, and expects to find positive responses from those with whom she interacts. The importance of relationships for her is evident in her drawings by the figures' large size and central position on the page. She gives great attention to showing each person's individuality with simple yet nuanced facial details, and gender-appropriate hair and clothing. Her drawing of her mother is especially notable for her large size and enlarged head and face, relative to the others. Emotion is strongly conveyed in this figure and in the others, as is the sense of the experience of her mother's ability to read and respond to her feelings and needs. Overall, her family drawings in childhood reveal robust, happy, open-armed parents and siblings, and a centered, open self-portrait of a happy little girl.

At age 18, Gail's figures are carefully detailed, in line with her superior cognitive skills and her reliance on intellectualization as a means of assuaging her adolescent anxieties. Her female and male figures appear to be stable, self-assured and positive, with wide eyes and full smiles. In her drawing of a girl, head to toe clothing, prominent bangs, and hands in pockets hint at Gail's shyness and discomfort with aspects of her physical self. Despite these anxieties, Gail portrays the sense of self and identity that allowed her to form and work towards her goals, indicated by the girl's open and positive face and posture.

A family drawing gives unique characteristics and roles to each member. Each family member has a clear relationship to the others, and different degrees and types of closeness and identification are apparent. While her physical self-consciousness is evident in her concealing of her own form in the drawing, Her emphasis on drawing herself with prominent hair and glasses points to her wish to be an individual, and to make her intellectual presence known. Gail's drawing of herself, conspicuously hidden behind male family members, suggest the feelings of having been "shut out" of the family that she expressed in her teenage years. This self-portrayal, like that of the female figure, speaks about Gail's difficulties in adolescence with feelings of physical and emotional vulnerability. Despite some physical insecurity, social discomfort, and conflict around asserting her own intellectual capacities, Gail's drawings convey a relatively emotionally aware, hopeful adolescent and a present and attuned sense of self, of others, and of relationships.

Synopsis

Both parents were strongly interested in our study throughout the time of our acquaintance. They were consistently thoughtful about Gail's behavior and let her know of the pride they felt in her development. Her mother was unusually competent and glad at the birth of this her third child. Gail had weathered several troubling periods in her first years, overcame them quietly and proceeded to develop well in all respects. Her story is retained here because it is distinctly at variance from the accounts of the other four children in this study.

CONFLICT AND EGO STRENGTH IN EARLY CHILDHOOD

4

Conflict and Ego Strength in Early Childhood

The dearth of parental understanding of children's behavior became ever more obvious in our study. Too few adults are aware of the impact of daily and hourly subjective experiences upon their infants and young children. Not enough children are helped or encouraged to describe their thoughts and feelings to their parents and to know they will be listened to. In general, adults are usually too preoccupied to consider the impact of the plethora of emotional and cognitive experiences in the young; it is as if children other than their own are colorless and their personalities too undeveloped to have any but short-term meaning. Many parents do not or cannot afford the time to think about what the young may be experiencing from day-to-day and hour-to-hour. Most fathers, far more than mothers, are at a loss as to how to describe their children; they can say how the children are doing in school, what physical illnesses they have had, and what entertainment they require. These are easy to report. Both parents are usually ready to describe advances in their children's physical abilities and aptitudes for language, but when asked about emotions they had observed in their children, although most were ready to report examples of what made their children happy (receiving gifts, eating ice cream, watching television) or unhappy (deprivation, punishment), they usually assumed that more subtle emotions such as longing, thoughtfulness, sadness, loneliness, or worry were rarely present in their children's first years. Adults may start families gladly, but with little idea of how to recognize and respond to experiences to come even in the immediate future, and usually they are unprepared to respond to common difficulties arising during early childhood. Usually, there are few opportunities for them to learn ahead of time about the emotional and cognitive needs of their young. The gaps in that learning have lain in a general disregard of children's affective experiences, especially those that arise during the second year of life, popularly identified as "the terrible twos," a designation that represents parental frustration about how to respond to the young child's rising declarations of independence. Much has to be learned by those in charge of the young about the immense possibilities for growth or growth failure observable in cognition, instinctual development, and object relatedness in early childhood. Until the past several decades, the first two to three years of life have been subject to few observations outside the home[20] unless the child has attended a nursery school or pre-school in which the faculty is composed of competent observers and communicators.

Problems of infant and child rearing are of course more intricate than a lack of parental information or goodwill. The readiness of many adults to rationalize or dismiss negative aspects of children's behavior usually reflects their own need to protect themselves from painful feelings of self-reproach for having made inadvertent but irrevocable mistakes in their child-rearing. The parents' conscience demands that they readily make clear to their children what they have done right or wrong, so that responsible parents are quick to impute "good" or "bad" behavior to the child, and, as seen in the reports above, many are also too ready to scold the misbehaviors that arouse parental anger, anxiety, or worry.

Some of the responsibility for having made mistakes in child rearing appears to be alleviated when it is displaced onto the child;

---

[20]Important exceptions have been appearing in the journal *Zero to Three* and in E. Furman's *Toddlers and Mothers* (1992).

in this way the parents project their self-reproach onto the child, and may become more punitive than they intended. Their self-reproach for their punitiveness may then give rise to their taking an unconstructively indulgent attitude towards their child. Fitting reprimands give a child an appreciation of having acted inappropriately, but excessive or unprovoked punishment wounds the nascent ego of the child. Such blows may be felt only vaguely, yet they can affect the quality of the child's self-regard. Excessive or hasty punishment is likely to arouse confusion in the child as to whether he or she has done something wrong or is an unworthy person. Such confusion may leave the child with a feeling that his or her honor is stained, and so may usher in too-loose or too-strict superego development in the child.

In the course of this study I was again and again troubled by the attitudes of many parents when referring to the disciplinary measures they took as giving the child "just one whack" or "just a few whacks." They rarely referred to "punishment." It appeared that in this way they were avoiding any idea that their "whacks" caused any pain, discomfort, or humiliation to the child. The slang word was used repeatedly as a way of referring to a natural and easy form of discipline, a simple reminder to the child to behave better.

Without an awareness of the effects of their behavioral mistakes, children have no motive to change their unfitting behavior and so may be left with no way of alleviating the stormy feelings it may have brought on. The deliverances of the superego are unconscious; unless the parents help the child become aware of its signals, they may create vague anxiety in the child who is only beginning to grasp the idea of that inner disquiet we call guilt. Two superegos are involved in the establishment of conscience in the child: one is that of the parent, who may reduce his or her own feelings of guilt by projecting them onto the child in their efforts to ensure that the child becomes responsible for his or her own actions. The other superego is the one developing in the child, who is not yet discerning enough to feel the difference between having done something that deserves blame and being a bad person. It takes time for this understanding to develop; in the process of cultivating a child's conscience a parent needs to be careful not to erode the child's early ego development.

Freud wrote far less about the component instincts than about libido and aggression, explaining that the component instincts are socially rather than biologically motivated. Given this, it may be surmised that the component instincts develop in accordance with the young child's earliest human relationships. Erikson (1950) charted eight stages of ego maturation or its failure, positing the development of Trust vs. Mistrust as the earliest stage, with later ego developments conditional to it, as follows:

1. (0-2[21]) Trust vs. Mistrust – e.g., Tina, Will
2. (2-4) Autonomy vs. Shame, Doubt – e.g., Lori
3. (4-6) Initiative vs. Guilt – e.g., Edwin
4. (7-11) Industry vs. Inferiority – e.g., Gail
5. (11-18) Identity vs. Role Diffusion (subjects not seen between ages 7 and 18)
6. Young Adulthood: Intimacy vs. Isolation[22]
7. Adulthood: Generativity vs. Stagnation
8. Maturity: Industry vs. Disgust, Despair

Erikson's primary placement of Trust v. Mistrust tells us that a newborn child's earliest social experiences are determined by relationships with his or her caregivers. When we compare Freud's statements about the development of the component instincts with Erikson's formulations, it becomes evident that the foundation of trust that is established between the parent and child in the first months or years of life affects the quality of the subsequent manifestations of the component instincts, which, as said before, are secondary and socially-determined. They may manifest themselves positively in a child who learns trust in his relationship to his primary caregivers.

Freud, being concerned with psychopathology, did not refer to the positive manifestations of the component instincts, noting only their negative appearances in his choice of their names: voyeurism, when it develops in a child whose sense of trust is sturdy, can be evident in his or her wholesome reach to gain knowledge through direct observation. The desire to look becomes synonymous with the desire to learn, but when a child consciously or unconsciously

---

[21]Approximate ages in years.
[22]Stages 6-8 do not pertain here because the subjects were not seen after age 18.

distrusts an elder, his or her inquisitiveness may become corrupted into the perversion of voyeurism. Similarly, exhibitionism may emerge in a child who doubts that he or she is worthy of another's notice, and may represent a silent crying out for someone to trust; a search that may decompose into a desperate attempt to attract notice by asking for confirmation of worth. Cruelty may be redefined as the negative end of a spectrum involving degrees of kindness. A child who trusts his or her parents is likely to manifest kindness in accordance with the kindness he or she has experienced, but a child filled with distrust is more apt to miss the development of kindness, with degrees of deliberate unkindness—cruelty—engendered in its place.

When we review the experiences of the children, we see how the qualitative development of each subject's component instincts varies according to their surrounding environments and their relationships with caregivers:

Subject 1: Lori's story demonstrates how voyeurism and exhibitionism are two sides of the same coin. She grew up in a setting where emotional comfort was almost always available without effort on her part, so her experience in developing frustration tolerance was minimal, which led her to a reliance on intrusive or exhibitionistic behaviors. In her early childhood, M played with Lori almost continuously, talking and singing to her and making faces for her to imitate. She kept trying to please Lori with social and physical games, praising her every act and sound. At three, Lori kept showing a need for M's attention, and if for a moment she lost it, she became restless, plaintive, and physically overactive; sometimes she screamed and sobbed, and often became upset to the point of vomiting. F said that Lori was tough, stubborn, not introspective, and refused to obey except when spoken to very sternly, which he rarely did. Proudly, he added, "She knows her own mind… she's never embarrassed… emotions do not get in her way." At four, Lori responded to tests poorly. At home she continued to be self-indulgent, asked excessively for M's help, and tried to get into the bathroom when M or grandmother were bathing in order to stare at their bodies.

When restricted, she tried to slap M. She cried in jealous distress when M put on something new or went out for social reasons. At five, her test responses were often excessive or irrelevant and she continued to show intense curiosity about genitalia. When any request was made of her, she expostulated, loudly talking about how mad she was, and played wildly until finally M spanked her. At school she demanded much attention from T, often complained that some part of her body hurt, wandered about imitating or interfering with other children, and was unable to occupy herself in any constructive way. At six, she continued to be disconcerted when uninvolved with others and was at a loss about what to do. At our office, she refused the usual test procedures, explaining that M had told her that she need not take the tests. M herself refused to come for her final interview, the only one of our full sample of 131 mothers to do so.

At eighteen, Lori showed little interest in responding to questions. Instead she acted silly or became distracted, doubted, and made guesses. She denounced her first high school exceedingly, then talked of the next school to which she had transferred, boasting of how its students were children of famous people from all over the world, yet again complained about teachers and unfair grades. She never expressed any self-criticism, but continually made references to herself. She mentioned the "mature" work that she did, how well she knew how to judge people, how many people and places she had heard about, complained about what irritated her, and gushed over things she found amusing. Always leaning forward as she spoke, she was constantly letting E know what she found important; to a great extent she spoke in platitudes.

Subject 2: Edwin's exhibitionism was mild and defensive, in that it reflected a desire to overcome or ignore anxiety. It appears to have been prompted by tensions experienced at home between his parents, and by F's overly strict discipline that stood out in stark contrast to his addiction to gambling. In his early childhood Edwin had shown a positive sensitivity to social demands; a few years later he began to prefer rough and noisy activities. At home he had a few unruly moments, but got over them quickly. His poor response to social demands appeared at school during rest periods in his behavior toward T and other children. He never avoided difficult tasks, but often whistled, hummed, or became rhetorical. At home he responded well to scientific projects, could play games by himself, and had become more self-assertive, especially toward F. At seven, he spoke and responded to tests excellently, but was at times restless. F's reports were brief and uninformative. He only recalled that Edwin became angry when he didn't get his way. M spoke to Edwin about his behavior without punishing him, so that he might understand why some of his actions were more or less acceptable. Whereas she tried to let the children settle their differences on their own, now and then F wanted them to stand at attention and confess.

At 18, Edwin presented himself as being quite secure. Although he had had to repeat ninth grade, he said it was no problem; he "just had not worked hard enough." He came out of high school with a C+ average, with which he was strangely content; his SAT scores were also very modest. He had no idea about future occupations, thought maybe he would like a desk job someday, then spoke a good deal about his close friends and his enjoyment of stories and magazines. Asked about himself, Edwin spoke mostly of boredom, which he thought was the worst feeling he could have; his main concern was to have fun with his friends. Of his brother Adam, Edwin said, "He just tries to be cool," which suggested a projection of Edwin's own feelings. He noted that F did not take pride in his work and that there was much tension at home because of F's gambling. He seemed to exaggerate his capacity to feel free; this may have caused him to obfuscate unhappy feelings stemming from F's addiction and apparent discontent. He had repetitive dreams of falling, again mentioned fears of being bored, and appeared to have developed superficial attitudes, pseudo self-satisfaction, and little drive toward achievement. Still, his personality was attractive because of the sincerity and integrity with which he gave his story. It was of interest that he expressed particular admiration for the Ten Commandments – "They cover everything," he said.

Subject 3: From earliest infancy Tina experienced little affection or understanding and endured almost uninterrupted disciplinary prodding to behave in ways she had never been helped by her parents to learn. A lack of real self-sufficiency led her to rely on exhibitionistic behaviors, often involving her unusual physical agility. Our earliest observations showed that, even then, she was overactive and difficult to manage. M's handling was rough and mechanical; she appeared to know no way to comfort Tina and several times told E that if E wanted, she "could have her." M thought the trouble was because of Tina's "personality"; she felt sure Tina was "spoiled." At age one, the child looked neglected. Her clothing was old and dirty and her legs were very bowed, yet her motor coordination was excellent. When M tried to dress her, she was so difficult that M became angry and had to "slap her legs or something like that," then they were often angry at each other. M looked shabby and unhappy. She seemed not to have given thought to reasons for Tina's behavior.

Tina liked to rush around her parents' store, picking up whatever was handy and so getting lots of attention from customers. In the early evening she would be taken upstairs by M's sister, then F played with the children, a few hours later M would come up to fix dinner. Then M and F went back to the store and Tina was left with her aunt to "play around" for hours, sometimes until midnight, before being put to bed by her aunt.

On arrival at two, Tina ran about the playroom handling objects haphazardly. In the store, she loved to clown and make people laugh, but with other children she kicked, pulled their hair, threw toys about, and showed off. M felt lost and overwhelmed by Tina's random and wild behavior; spanking, although a regular part of each day, was not a reliable deterrent. At three, Tina rejected almost all test items. F told of how easily Tina was bored and how much she wanted to keep talking about everything that had happened or would happen. When asked by her parents to do something, she kicked, screamed, hit, and threw things. At four, her speech was very immature and her estimated IQ on the Stanford-Binet was 103 (it was difficult to know how accurate this score was). In school her hands and her clothing were very dirty, her hair was a mess, and she jumped from one activity to another. If T stayed by her she was much more able to focus her efforts effectively. At five she arrived looking malnourished, with her face dirty and her clothing soiled. Her vocabulary was very poor, and her speech startlingly vulgar. M again reported her worries about Tina's disobedience; when not allowed to wear what she wanted, she yelled and sometimes hit M. When it was time to leave our office Tina became obstreperous. The next year it was not long before M and Tina began arguing or bossing each other. Tina continued her acrobatics, watching E as if to make sure she was being watched. At home she now slept with M every night, not wanting a blanket but putting her legs on top of M (did she need to make sure M stayed close?). Now Tina had many chores at home. M seemed apathetic, complaining about disciplining Tina's stubbornness and defiance as though such difficulties were problematic for herself, not for Tina. M and F could not consider private school for the children, said M, because that would mean the parents "would be spending all their money on the children." Tina's behavior in school now seemed more appropriate; in helping two boys fix a disorderly situation, it turned out that she was identifying more with T than with the boys. About school, she complained, "They should clean up the stuff they play with." Asked to think of something pleasant, she said, "Clean up the world – clean up the streets and help everybody" (at age five she had also seemed to fixate on dirtiness, drawing a picture of soap; at home there must have been much talk about being clean or dirty). M was still pleased that Tina was "aggressive" and "said funny things."

At eighteen during psychological tests anxiety interfered with all of Tina's responses. She relied on trial and error, her thinking was over-personalized, and she often retreated to fantasy and confabulations. Her thinking had become somewhat paranoid, deteriorating while under stress. She appeared to have pathetically little self-esteem and showed an intense need to be attached to a stronger person. There were many indications of her being afraid of F and needing to align herself with M, and she appeared overwhelmed by her inability to respond to everyday demands. She had not achieved any positive social relationships; she tried to explain this as a result of her having so many chores at home, which were indeed excessive. She glossed over the importance of difficulties, only wishing that the family "were more like a classic kind of family," and was now angry at her parents for having little interest in her life or her future. They did not "appreciate [her] potentials." She described every aspect of her life as if it were dull or unimportant, except for tennis. Her life experience was constricted; she had few stable relationships with family or friends.

Subject 4: From the time Will was an infant, his M felt uneasy about recognizing his needs. He appeared to have received no emotional comfort or guidance, which must have brought on feelings of tension, apprehension, and isolation. Perhaps his early abuse of other children which had begun as a function of his confusion over how to behave then became a way for him to gain a sense of power that he otherwise lacked. The severity of his conflicts did not become obvious to his parents until he was much older. As far as we could tell, they never offered advice about how to change his aggressive behavior. By the end of his early childhood, he appeared to have converted confusion and longing into a front of control and self-sufficiency.

Early on, Will experienced little communication, spending much time alone. M did not know how to respond to his crying or his hunger and often left him alone to cry himself to sleep. Most of the time he slept or cried, or was extremely restless. He became disinterested in food, which might be attributed in part to his having been given the bottle in complete silence. By age two, he quickly responded to test objects, then as quickly threw them away. He always liked to watch children play, but when close to them tried to pull their hair – it was as if he longed to reach out but had no idea of how to do so. M didn't know what to do about "discipline," but said she liked to watch Will as he slept, because "he looked so sweet," and she could sit back and do nothing. When he was twenty-one months his brother Lewis was born; Will soon began to scream at, hit, and play roughly with him, or he asked M to take Lewis away. At three, Will was continually fretful. His desire for his bottle had become more intense, not only all day but during the night and on waking in the morning. With other children he became overexcited, frustrated, or angry. After he bit Lewis' finger, F simply deprived him of his "usual daily gifts." F realized that giving Will a bottle in order to have him fall asleep was convenient for his parents. At age four, during tests, Will often spoke too quickly and in long elaborate sentences, mumbled, sometimes burst into tears, or made up answers at random. He did not like nursery school because there were "too many children" there, and cried so much that his parents thought it best to withdraw him from school. His eating habits were poor; he always wanted to leave the table as soon as possible (when he did not eat, his parents told him to leave the table.) He still loved going to bed because it meant getting his bottle. After using the toilet, he feared the sound of the toilet flushing and wanted M to stay with him, a demand with which she complied. Outdoors, he was angered by any restrictions and had many tantrums; M "could not get through to him." She thought he now had a fear of the dark triggered by "accidentally" hurting his brother. Another time, when Will accidentally broke his brother's finger, Will told his parents that Lewis "knocked the table over on himself," a statement they did not question. F said that "for some curious reason" Will just couldn't stand school, showed wild and selfish behavior and "batter[ed]" other children. F then acknowledged that he had no idea how to handle Will's recklessness.

At five, Will entered the office with reluctance, fearfully refused to look at or speak to E and stayed physically close to M. When testing began he became excited and succeeded with genuine pleasure and pride, often boasting of his performance, then became uneasy and did not engage in any tests that required the use of both hands. When challenged by some of the tests he quickly made excuses, rationalizing his difficulty with irrelevant statements such as, "I can't look at it closely because my eyes are blinking." When school began he demanded that M stay with him and after two weeks; when she wished not to, he fell into such a panic that he had to be taken to the director's office and was later brought home. M mentioned that she thoroughly enjoyed the children's being away from home in the afternoons. Will still needed a nightlight to fall asleep and was often kept awake by "bad thoughts" that he was unable to explain. In the mornings he liked to run wild in his play and he always liked to imagine that he was very strong and could do anything; actually, he became hysterical over small obstacles. M thought he got into trouble with children "just for the fun of fighting." There were run-ins at home when Will hit M or Lewis, scattered toys all over the apartment, and used crayons to draw all over the walls. When frustrated he scratched and picked at his body. Temper tantrums occurred daily. At night, he tossed, turned, sometimes talked unintelligibly, and often awoke with nightmares. F hoped that Will would learn to adapt to school "without breaking himself up."

At six, Will entered the office wordlessly, looking miserable. That morning, M had called to cancel his appointment, explaining that he had a 103-degree fever. Puzzlingly, she called again an hour later to say that he was all right and that they would come. She appeared impassive; silence prevailed during M-C activity, and at the end of it Will made the dolls strike each other repeatedly. He responded to test questions incorrectly, and when confronted with difficult items said, "I don't know." He rationalized failures on tests he had passed a year ago, behaved condescendingly toward E, and left at the end of testing without a word. M said that at school he had periods of "going berserk"; there was now much trouble at home with his aggressiveness, and there were frequent spankings. At school he did not eat lunch; M did not question this because, "He always ate bread and milk and didn't starve." A second brother, Seth, was born; soon Will spoke morosely at school of "babies with their dirty diapers," surely a projection of his own continuing difficulties in being toilet trained. At seven, Will refused all psychological tests and said he hated first grade. M spoke of many facets of his immaturity that she could not explain, such as his constant need for his security blanket, the odd requirement of a sleeping bag on top of his bed during the night, his nightly visits to the kitchen for some food or drink, the urging and help he needed in the morning to get dressed, and his frequent returns from school with wet pants. M only urged him to be more careful. He liked rough play, teased his brothers, talked a lot about crime, and told M he would never have children because they were "too much trouble." M could not think of anything that made him feel guilty and thought he had no fears. Seriously, she commented that he would either turn out to be a "great person" or a "terrific criminal." Whenever he visited another child's home, he became frustrated and angry. F thought Will had "a modest amount of self-control, considering his temperament," adding that he admired the child's rebelliousness. He said Will probably had needed more structure when he was younger, but that even if he (F) could do things over again, he would not have been able to provide it.

When Will was eighteen, M said he didn't want to come for the interview and certainly would not take any tests. On the telephone, he let me know that he might not keep any appointments he made because he might have something else he would rather do, then agreed to come and dictated the exact day and hour he would meet me. His school, he said, was informal—"There's never any work." He didn't wish to attend, but it was all right because there was a lot of freedom. He was highly critical of the teachers, except for one whom F had known, and said he was ahead of all the other students in his class. When he was younger he had refused to go to school and had stayed away until sixth grade, so his parents had taken him to a psychiatrist, to whom he had refused to speak. He rejected a second psychiatrist's prescription for an antidepressant. After a third doctor also prescribed antidepressants, Will and his parents became frightened; he "decided to become normal." He went back to high school for three years (after having stayed away from school for seven) and did well, but was still in conflict with classmates. He resumed criticizing the school staff and the subjects of study, spoke condescendingly of his teachers' ignorance, and boasted that he never understood any of the subjects; he only "memorized enough to pass tests easily." He was highly judgmental of colleges to which he applied, had no idea of what he wished to do in the future and thought the question was silly; on the SATs he earned a 650 in Math and a 790 in Verbal.

He went to sports games and concerts with friends and enjoyed reading science fiction and spy stories, and about music, weapons, and armor. With his parents he liked to go to concerts and lectures about society and ethics. He had almost no good memories of his childhood. He had disliked the school library, where no talking was allowed: "It's not that you're disturbing anybody, but you're communicating in their library, and that bothers them." Most television, he said, "was garbage," adding that he knew such remarks were excessive, then asserted that he never lost his temper about anything: "It's better strategically to keep calm." Most of all he seemed to express self-satisfaction. His conscience didn't bother him, he said, because he did not do anything to bother it. Asked whether he would want to change himself in any way, he said no, that he "only wanted to have more fun," then lightly expressed a wish to have been able to "behave normally" at school. He complained of always feeling hungry, said he was glad to have a snack at our office, then mentioned that there was no point in the tests given there; he did not want to be asked to do "purposeless things." He had complained of a music teacher who knew nothing about music theory; later, when asked about learning to play the piano, he contradicted himself and said he was not interested in theory. At the close of the interview, asked to take a simple sentence completion test, he surveyed it, put it down, and said, "No. I just don't want to." He appeared to have intense affect hunger that had to be denied absolutely and to find safety in indicating his sovereignty over anyone who might have any authority whatsoever.

Subject 5: Gail showed no wholly negative aspects of the component instincts posited by Freud. It may be of benefit here to ponder just what role the component instincts play in the development of "normal" behavior. It could be that Gail never displayed any negative extremes of voyeurism, exhibitionism, or cruelty because of her sensitivity to the regulating power of social normalcy, or because her environment was somehow wholesome enough to keep the negative aspects of the component instincts in check. Further probing beyond these general explanations might show that the component instincts have a deeper and heretofore unexplored positive role in the development of all children as they work out the tensions regarding the need to inquire into unknown subjects (voyeurism), the need to be seen and heard (exhibitionism), and the need to establish one's integrity (cruelty). The space where the component instincts develop in a child may be seen as a kind of open field for the reverberation of tensions (as a child approaches new frontiers with both fear and excitement). When the child begins to mature these open fields may narrow, becoming manifest in tendencies toward positive or negative social behaviors, moderate or extreme, depending on the child's individual experience.

Gail traveled through the early stages of development with no significant setbacks in spite of early visual problems and the teasing about them that she experienced in school. At age eight she was found to have some astigmatism in one eye and for a period had worn an eye patch. At eighteen, when asked about anything that troubled her during her childhood, she responded, "You mean beside my eyes?" then added, "My hair, of course." She used to spend hours brushing it and "still had difficulty." Then she mentioned her belief in ghosts; it appeared to contain a mixture of anxiety and interest. Being talkative, she went on to say that if she didn't believe in an afterlife she would feel guilt, then mentioned a past fear of heights. Abundant speech and emphasis on moral behavior suggested a hidden anxiety about impulsivity not unusual in adolescents. She then remembered that in her childhood she often became silly or preachy, but had been able to control this tendency. She also sucked her thumb almost all of the time until age eight. After relating all of these "faults," she said that she had always been at ease socially and was noted to be calm, good-natured, introspective, and rarely upset, except if she saw people's feelings being hurt. "I've always been against injustice," she said.

The Superego, Trust, and Maturation

Each of Erikson's eight stages of ego maturation is dependent on the resolution of the tensions within the stage that came before it. Following this logic, the first stage, Trust v. Mistrust, is an important starting point: trust, mistrust, or distrust of the parent are instrumental to the growth of the child's superego; here we may see connections between ego and superego weakness and a pathological development of the component instincts. The superego alerts the child against socially unacceptable looking, drawing of attention, or cruel behavior, but when a paucity of trust has led to an underdeveloped superego, such interdiction fails to occur. In undisturbed cases, the component instincts are regulated under the watchful eye of the superego, since their manifestation involves a choice (or a decided lack of choice) between actions. Voyeurism would appear to be a relatively passive perversion; it seems to involve looking only and so may be regarded as somewhat milder in force than the other component instincts. The eyes, however, are essentially active; voyeurism thus involves the will to notice, imbibe, grasp, look intrusively, take in or absorb, and in all of these ways it is within the superego's influence as an active instinct. Exhibitionism, although it may involve a more passive request to be looked at, is more physically active in its gathering of attention. It includes acts of showing off, attracting attention, and aiming to receive admiration. Voyeurism and exhibitionism often occur in tandem. Cruelty involves specific aggression enacted against objects with the wish to hurt or destroy. Its pathological manifestation is both more severe and more reprehensible than that of voyeurism or exhibitionism. After early childhood, cruelty is apt to find expression in the perversions of sadism and masochism.

In re-examining the subjects in light of Erikson's eight stages of ego maturation, we find that during infancy Tina and Will both encountered complications in the first phase of ego development, Trust v. Mistrust. They must have suffered a wounded sense of trust and a consequent loss of confidence in their mothers, and later in both parents' with their irregular enforcement of rules, leading to confused superego development. Tina encountered complications as she began to distrust her parents in response to their absence of affection and their overzealous punishments, leading to her loss of feelings of integrity. Her deficient autonomy and impoverished capacity to think and to socialize led to her poor ego strength. Will's mother did not know how to respond to his needs, leaving him in a world of his own that contained very little comfort or education. His distrust and anger must have been central to the aggravation of his hostile behavior – in sum, he appeared to have kicked libido aside and embraced aggression.

In contrast to Will and Tina, Lori's difficulty stemmed from an excess of parental indulgence, leading to problems in Erikson's second stage of ego development, Autonomy v. Shame, Doubt. As she matured, closely absorbed ties to her mother led Lori to an overly intense sense of trust that came to be shadowed by self-doubt. Burdened by identification with M's excessive show of self-satisfaction and leaning on M as a perpetual crutch, Lori compensated for a lack of autonomy, hid her shame behind exhibitionistic behavior, and so was hindered from developing integrity. She became impelled to look at others obtrusively or invasively and lacked self-sustaining initiative.

In Erikson's stage three, Initiative v. Guilt, Edwin encountered conflict. Until age five he had developed very well, with industry and with pride in his intelligence. He must have felt confusion over parental examples, however, about what he should do with his initiative: F's discontent, disinterest in his work, failure to give adequate attention to the needs of his family, as well as the overall tensions between his parents, must have brought confusion. Caught between identification with F's self-interest and a sense of its effects on M, Edwin encountered difficulty in progress to Erikson's fourth stage, Industry v. Inferiority, and was halted by resignation to the latter. Tina, Will, Cora, and Edwin had all, by the start of adolescence, developed problems with their motivation and their sense of identity. Gail, in contrast, traveled through these early stages of development with no significant disturbance. She retained a wholesome trust in both parents, who had shown unequivocal interest in her activities and growing independence. She developed autonomy, showed initiative in her schooling, and was able to maintain balanced social relationships. At eighteen, she was preparing to enter a first-rate college, had excellent relationships with her parents, siblings, and friends, and was aspiring toward the study of rhetoric (which might represent a sublimation of the over-eager speech of her childhood) and law.

The significance of the component instincts lies in their stress on good object relationships and engagement in good work.

To highlight the importance of the child's trust in his earliest caregivers, I emphasize the role played by simple affection in the establishment of that trust by an example: My friend Galina told me how she sat on a park bench on a summer day with her sister, the sister's one-year-old baby sitting between them. As the two adults chatted, Galina gently placed her hand on the baby's head, caressing it softly for a few moments, then replaced her hand in her lap. A few seconds later, the baby reached for her aunt's hand, picked it up, and placed it back on her own head. In effect, she was saying, "I like it, do it more," which her aunt then gladly did. This is a very small instance of the value of an adult's wordless expression of loving-kindness to an infant. In such transient ways can an infant take an active part in building trust in an adult.

APPENDIX A:
PSYCHOLOGICAL TESTS
ADMINISTERED

Appendix A: Psychological Tests Administered

IN-TEXT ABBREVIATION	NOTES	AGE(S) ADMINISTERED AT
	Merril-Palmer Scale of Mental Intelligence	2-3
Stanford-Binet	Revised Form L-M (scores not reliable prior to age 4)	3-7
WISC	Wechsler Intelligence Scale for Children	3-7
	Draw-a-Man	4
M-C Play	Mother-Child Play interaction (administered prior to psychological tests)	4, 5
	Graham-Ernhart Block Sorting	4-5
CAT	Children's Apperception Test	2-7
	Draw-a-Person, Draw-Your-Family	5
WPPSI	Wechsler Primary and Preschool Scale of Intelligence	5
Piaget Tasks	Volume Judgement based on water displacement	5-7
TAT	Thematic Apperception Test	6, 7, 18
WRAT	Wide Range Achievement Test	7
Rorschach		7, 18
WAIS-R	Wechsler Adult Intelligence Scale-Revised	18

APPENDIX B:
INTERVIEW FORM: MOTHER AND FATHER, AGE 7

Appendix B: Interview Form: Mother and Father, Age 7

I. School Attendance

1. First or second grade? Public, private, or parochial? During past year, did C (child) have any sort of troubles in connection with school? Any special successes? Is M now satisfied with school set-up? With teacher?

2. How does C like school, generally? To what does he look forward most of all in school? Anything he doesn't like there? Does he show any reluctance to go to school? If so, how often? Or when? Has he become more interested in learning to read or write letters and numbers, outside of school? Did he know the whole alphabet when he entered first grade? (If not: Does he know it now? Do you think he is likely to become a "reader?"

3. What does M hope C can accomplish this year in school, in addition to learning regular work of his grade?

II. Family Events
   A. New sibling?
      1. Date of birth. Pregnancy and delivery untroubled?
      2. C's reactions to these events?
      3. Does M think C expressed his true reactions to her?

   B. Residence: Any changes? Bedroom arrangements? M's and C's attitudes if any changes have occurred?

   C. Parents and siblings: any events of possible importance or interest to C, e.g., separations, long vacations, illnesses or accidents, work problems?

III. Health and Physical Functions
  A. (omit from interview with F) Present height and weight? Date when these measures were taken?

  B. Illness, surgical procedures or accidents? Chronic conditions? If any, what were C's reactions to events and to medical care? M's reactions?

  C. Food
    1. Appetite: any changes during the past year? Old problems remaining? Or any new ones? If so, how handled?
    2. In general, is appetite more or less than formerly?
    3. Meals with whom? Table manners adequate?
    4. Are there any problems? (i.e., dawdling, restlessness)?

  D. Sleep
    1. Bedtime hours? Usual bedtime procedure? How much of it can C manage alone? Any dawdling, resistances? How handled?
    2. Dreams reported often? Nightmares? Examples? How handled?
    3. Any sleep problems occurring during night or in early morning? Changes in past year? If any problems, how handled?
    4. Usual morning routine? Waking hour?

  E. Toileting
    1. Any periods of constipation or diarrhea? Cause? How handled?
    2. In case of enuresis: any changes in pattern during past year? M's and C's present attitudes? Plan regarding handling?

3. Any other bowel or bladder difficulty? If so, inquire again regarding attitudes, present or prospective handling.
4. Does C use toilet in school?

F. Grooming
1. Has resistance to cleanliness (hands, face, bath) increased? Does C ever bathe with anyone else in the family? With whom? How does he feel about being seen nude? Is he curious about seeing anyone else undressed?
2. Any help needed or asked for in bath? In dressing?
3. Is he more (still) interested in choosing his own clothing? How about clothes-consciousness this year?

IV. Social Behavior
A. In Family
1. Has his relationship to anyone in the family, or to the family in general changed during past year? Does he admire anyone in particular? Get bothered by anyone in particular?
2. Usually, at home, is he an easy C to get along with? Or is he one who often needs to be "handled with care?" (If reply is that nothing bothers him, ask:) Isn't there anything that might put him in a bad mood?

B. With Children Outside Family
1. Does he have any steady friendships now? Any preference for boys or girls? Older or younger C's? After school hours, does he prefer to be outdoors, or at home, or at the homes of friends? Doing what? Does he go to other children's homes as readily as he wants them to come to his (or vice versa)? Is he more comfortable with one C or a group?
2. Does he prefer to take the lead in doing things with Cs or would he just as lief take their suggestions? (If answer is "Both," ask:) What makes the difference? His mood?

The C he happens to be with? The activity?

3. In what kind of situations is he most likely to run into trouble with other Cs? Does he then want help from adults? Or does he usually settle matters by himself?(If answer is that he usually has no trouble, ask:) Doesn't he ever get into any big fights or quarrels?(If answer is that he is always getting into trouble, ask:) Doesn't he ever get along pleasantly with other Cs?

4. How does he react to teasing? (If necessary: I mean teasing that might hurt his feelings—not mere joking.) Or does he like to do the teasing—if so, whom does he tease, and how?

5. Winning games usually becomes important at about this age: how is it with C if he loses? Some C's just want to quit, some get angry, some try to change the rules—what does C do? (ask kind of game). Cheating in games also happens more often at this age: Does M know if C does? Or does he accuse others of cheating?(Where appropriate ask:) Doesn't he ever seem to mind losing? And when he wins, does he ever boast about it? (Where appropriate ask:) Is it the same if he plays games with adults?

C. With Adults

1. Are there any adults whom he now especially wants to be with, or admires? Any whom he definitely dislikes?

2. In general, do you think that C is more comfortable with adults or with Cs now?

V. Sublimation

A. Work and Activity

1. Can you name just two or three things C likes to spend his time at most of all? (if appropriate:) Typically, does he prefer to do these things with others?

2. Are there ever times when he is at loose ends, and can't

find anything to do? Does he accept suggestions easily?

3. Cs of this age often develop special hobbies, like collecting things, or dressing up, or learning about al or the baseball players—has C any such interest? If so, does he keep his interest long enough to get satisfaction from it? (Months? Weeks? Days? Hours?)

4. What household chores or jobs does he have to do regularly? Is he responsible about carrying them out?

5. Does he have any favorite TV programs or TV characters? How much TV does he watch daily now? More or less than when younger? M's attitude toward amount and kind of viewing.

6. Most Cs dislike or don't enjoy some activities. Do you know which ones C doesn't care for?

B. Knowledge and Thinking

1. Ideas about law, governments, or justice often begin to be expressed more when children begin grade school. Can you recall any things he has said or questions he has asked about law-breaking, or crime, or punishments?

2. What about other interests expressed in past year: (for each, if answer is yes, ask how shown and where appropriate, how handled by M): Money?* Future work? Marriage and family? God and religion? Birth? Death? War? Any other social problem (racism, pollution, wildlife conservation)?

3. Has he expressed any new aspiration or ambition? (If yes:) which?

VI. Character Traits

A. Independence

1. How much reminding does C need to follow through on daily routines of his own (getting to places on time, picking up possessions, knowing where his own things are)?

2. Is he much of a "forgetter?" Does he lose things often? In general, do you consider him responsible enough for a C of his age?
3. Some Cs at seven seem almost too independent. Have you noticed any changes since last year in his assertiveness, or defiance? Or even rebelliousness? M's attitudes (may be implicit in her response)?
4. How does he react now to frustrations or disappointments? Can he accept compromises? How upset does he get?
5. (Where appropriate:) Doesn't he ever make a fuss for something he wants very much? (If answer is no:) Do you think of this trait as something helpful to him or do you wish he might react differently?
6. What do you think C likes about himself? How do you know? Dislikes? How do you know?

B. Control v. Impulsivity:
1. Do you think he is able (no, in comparison to the past) to make good judgments about his own behavior—for example, can he stop himself from doing things that might be dangerous or foolish? Does he tend to rush into action without thinking about results or is he rather likely to be over cautious?
2. Do you think of him as patient, generally, or is he liable to get irritated when he has to cope with delays?
3. Discipline: is C getting to need more or less? For what? Usual methods? (If any physical punishment is mentioned, ask:) About how often is that necessary? e.g. how many times a week might it be necessary?
4. In general, do you think C has achieved enough self-control for a C of seven? Are there any ways in which you would wish him to have more? (Or: to let down a bit?)

C. Affect
1. If you had to choose just one or two adjectives (words)

to describe C's most characteristic moods, which would you choose? (If necessary: e.g., serious, calm, overactive, lazy).

2. For each of the following, ask: "What situations make him _____?" And for all but first three, seek details, if possible, regarding intensity or frequency, e.g., "Does he stay sad long?" "How often does he get that angry?")

3. Happy? Sad? Shy? Worried? Angry?

4. How does he take criticism now? (ignore? Fight? Listen? Joke?)

5. When he has done something he himself believes is wrong, can he admit it? Does he seem ashamed? Or is he likely to place the blame for his action on others?

6. How about his reactions to punishment now (as above)?

7. Have you been aware of any stealing at all? Or attempts to steal? Most Cs do some at about the time they are learning to count and to handle numbers. Some try to "collect" money, some try to pilfer other little things at home, or in their friends' homes.

8. (If yes:) Can he admit it? How did you (do you) handle the problem? Are you at all concerned about it?

9. How about lying?—which is also a frequent development at age seven. (If yes:) In what situations? Can he admit it? How handled?

10. Are there any other things that ever make him act guilty? Does he often express such feelings? In general, do you think of him as having a strict conscience, or a lenient conscience? (If answer is, "It depends," ask for examples of what C might be strict about, what lax about.)

VII. Other Signs of Disturbance
   A. Habits at present? Which are the ones noticed most recently> M's and C's attitudes? How handled? Any concerns for effects in the future?

B. Fears at present? Which are the ones you've noticed most recently> Do you think any fears which C had in the past have had any effect upon his development?

C. Does C have any character traits that worry M? (If yes:) Does M have any ideas as to what could help change this? Or could have helped prevent it?(or, how you might have avoided it?)

VIII.General impressions of M about Child
A. What character traits of C please M especially? Does M have any idea about what these good developments should be attributed to?

B. In what areas, if any, do you think he needs most development? Would she do anything differently if she could do it over again? (If yes:) does M think she had enough information about babies and Children during C's development? (If no:) What kinds of information would have been helpful

IX. Write a brief description of M. Note any changes of appearance, expressive behavior, expressed attitudes toward C, apparent attitude to interviewer.

REFERENCES

References

Abraham, K. (1908), The psychological relations between sexuality and alcoholism. *Selected Papers of Karl Abraham*, Third Impression. London: Hogarth Press, 1948, pp.80-89.
— (1916), The first pregenital stage of the libido. *Selected Papers of Karl Abraham*, Third Impression. London: Hogarth Press, 1948, pp.248-279.
— (1924), The influence of oral erotism on character formation. *Selected Papers of Karl Abraham*, Third Impression. London: Hogarth Press, 1948, pp.393-406.

Abrams, S. (1990), The psychoanalytic process: the developmental and the integrative. *Psychoanalytic Quarterly*, 59:650-667.

Arlow, J. (1981), Theories of pathogenesis. *Psychoanalytic Quarterly*, 50:488-514.

Bornstein, B. (1935), Phobia in a two-and-a-half year-old. *Psychoanalytic Quarterly*, 4:93-118.
— (1948), Emotional barriers in the understanding and treatment of children. *American Journal of Orthopsychiatry*, 18:691-697.
— (1951), On latency. *Psychoanalytic Study of the Child*, 6:279-285.
— (1953), Masturbation in the latency period. *Psychoanalytic Study of the Child*, 8: 65-78.

Bowlby, J. (1960), Separation anxiety. *International Journal of*

Psycho-Analysis, 41:89-113.

Brody, S. (1956), *Patterns of Mothering*. New York: International Universities Press.
— (1960), Self-rocking in infancy. *Journal of the American Psychoanalytic Association*, 8:464-491.
— (1970), A mother is being beaten: an instinctual derivative and infant care. *Parenthood: Its Psychology and Psychopathology*, E.J. Anthony & T. Benedek (eds.). Boston: Little Brown, pp.427-447.
— (1974), The contribution of Berta Bornstein to child analysis. *Psychoanalytic Study of the Child*, 29: 13-20.
— (1980), Transitional objects: idealization of a phenomenon. *Psychoanalytic Quarterly*, 49:561-605.
— (1982), Psychoanalytic theories of infant development and its disturbances: A critical evaluation. *Psychoanalytic Quarterly*, 51:516-597.
— (2002, rev. 2007), The Development of Anorexia Nervosa: The Hunger Artists. Madison, CT: International Universities Press.

Brody, S. & Axelrad, S. (1970), *Anxiety and Ego Formation in Infancy*. New York: International Universities Press.
— (1978), *Mothers, Fathers, and Children: Explorations in the Formation of Character in the First Seven Years*. New York: International Universities Press.

Brody, S. & Siegel, M. (1992), *The Evolution of Character*. New York: International Universities Press.

Buhler, C. (1935), *From Birth to Maturity*. London: Routledge and Kegan Paul.

Buhler, K. (1919), *The Mental Development of the Child*. London: Routledge and Kegan Paul, 1930.

Call, J.D. (1964), Newborn approach behavior and early ego development. *International Journal of Psycho-Analysis*, 45:286-293.

— (1968), Lap and Finger Play in Infancy, Implications for Ego Development. *International Journal of Psycho-Analysis*, 49:325-378.

— (1980), Some prelinguistic aspects of language development. *Journal of the American Psychoanalytic Association*, 28:259-289.

Claparéde, E. (1913), *Experimental Pedagogy and the Psychology of the Child*. London: Edward Arnold.

Compton, A. (1981). On the psychoanalytic theory of instinctual drives, I: The beginnings of Freud's Drive Theory. *Psychoanalytic Quarterly*, 50:190-218.

Darwin, C. (1955). *The Expression of Emotions in Man and Animals*. New York: Philosophical Library.

Emde, R.M. (1984), *The Affective Self: Continuities and Transformations from Infancy*. Frontiers of Infant Psychiatry, J.D. Call, E. Galenson, and R. Tyson (eds.), Vol. 2. New York: Basic Books.

Emde, R.M., Gaensbauer, T.J., & Harmon, R.J. (1970), *Emotional Expression in Infancy*. Psychological Issues, Monograph 37. New York: International Universities Press.

Erikson, E. H. (1950), *Childhood and Society*. New York: W. W. Norton & Company.

Fenichel, O. (1945), *The Psychoanalytic Theory of Neurosis*. New York: W.W. Norton.

Ferenczi, S. (1913), Stages in the Development of the Sense of Reality. *First Contributions to Psychoanalysis*, London: Hogarth Press, pp.212-239.

Freud, A. (1945), Indications for child analysis. *Writings of Anna Freud, IV: Indications for Child Analysis and Other Papers, 1945-1956*. New York: International Universities Press, 1968, pp.3-38.

— (1954), Problems with Infantile Neurosis: Contribution to the Discussion. *Writings of Anna Freud, IV: Indications for Child Analysis and Other Papers, 1945-1956*. New York: International Universities Press, 1968, pp.327-355.

— (1965), *Normality and Pathology in Childhood: Assessments of Development*. New York: International Universities Press, pp.62-107.

— (1967), Residential vs. foster care. *Writings of Anna Freud, VII: Problems of Psychoanalytic Training, Diagnosis, and the Technique of Therapy, 1966-1970*. New York: International Universities Press, 1971, pp.223-239.

— (1970a), The Symptomatology of Childhood: A Preliminary Attempt at Classification. *Writings of Anna Freud, VII: Problems of Psychoanalytic Training, Diagnosis, and the Technique of Therapy, 1966-1970*. New York: International Universities Press, 1971, pp.157-188.

— (1970b), The Infantile Neurosis: Genetic and Dynamic Considerations. *Writings of Anna Freud, VII: Problems of Psychoanalytic Training, Diagnosis, and the Technique of Therapy, 1966-1970*. New York: International Universities Press, 1971, pp.189-203.

— (1974), A Psychoanalytic View of Developmental Psychopathology. *Writings of Anna Freud, VIII: Psychoanalytic Psychology of Normal Development, 1970-1980*. New York: International Universities Press, 1981, pp.57-74.

Freud, A. & Burlingham, D. (1943), *War and Children*. New York: Medical War Books.

Freud, S. (1905), Three essays on infantile sexuality. *Standard Edition*, 7: 130-243. London: Hogarth Press, 1953.
— (1908), Character and anal erotism. *Standard Edition*, 19:167-176. London: Hogarth Press, 1959.
— (1909), Notes upon a case of obsessional neurosis. *Standard Edition*, 10:155-249. London: Hogarth Press, 1955.
— (1912), Totem and taboo. *Standard Edition*, 13:1-162. London: Hogarth Press, 1955.
— (1914), On narcissism: an introduction. *Standard Edition*, 14:73-102. London: Hogarth Press, 1957.
— (1915), Instincts and their vicissitudes. *Standard Edition*, 14:109-140. London: Hogarth Press, 1957.
— (1920), Beyond the pleasure principle. *Standard Edition*, 18:1- 64. London: Hogarth Press, 1955.
— (1923) The ego and the id. *Standard Edition*, 21:13-48. London: Hogarth Press, 1961.
— (1927), The future of an illusion. *Standard Edition*, 21:5-56. London: Hogarth Press, 1961.
— (1930), Civilization and its discontents. Standard Edition, 21:64-145, 1961. London: Hogarth Press, 1961

Furman, E. (1992), *Toddlers and their Mothers*. Madison, Connecticut: International Universities press.

Hanly, C. (1978), Instincts and hostile affects. *International Journal of Psychoanalysis*, 59:149-156.
— (1978), A critical consideration of Bowlby's ethological theory of anxiety. *Psychoanalytic Quarterly*, 47:364-380.
— (1978), The concept of truth in psychoanalysis. *International Journal of Psychoanalysis*, 71:375-383.

Hartmann, H. (1939), *Ego Psychology and the Problem of Adaptation*. New York: Holms.

— (1952), The mutual influences in the development of ego and id. *Psychoanalytic Study of the Child*, 7: 9-30.

Kagan, J. (1996), Three pleasing ideas. *American Psychologist*, 51:901-958.

Keller, H. (1903), *The Story of My Life*. New York: Doubleday.

Klein, M. (1921), The development of a child. *Love, Guilt, and Reparation, & Other Works, 1921-1945*. New York: Delacorte Press/Seymour Lawrence, pp.1-53.

— (1928), Early stages of the Oedipus conflict. *Contributions to Psycho-Analysis, 1921-1945*. London: Hogarth Press, 1948, pp.215-226.

— (1930), The importance of symbol-formation in the development of the ego. *Contributions to Psycho-Analysis, 1921-1945*. London: Hogarth Press, 1948, pp.236-250.

— (1936), Weaning. *On the Bringing Up of Children*, Rickman (ed.). London: Kegan Paul.

— (1952), On observing the behaviour of young infants. *Envy and Gratitude, & Other Works, 1946-1963*. New York: Delacorte Press/Seymour Lawrence pp.94-121.

Kroeber, A.L. (1925), The Yurok. *Handbook of the Indians of California*. Bureau of American Ethnology, Bulletin 78.

Leach, P. (1977), *Your Baby & Child: From Birth to Age Five*. New York: Knopf.

Levin, R. (1986), Infantile omnipotence and grandiosity. *Psychoanalytic Review*, 73: 57-76.

Lewin, B.D. (1950b), Addenda to the Theory of Oral Eroticism. Selected Writings of Bertram D. Lewin, J.A. Arlow (ed.). New York: *Pyschoanalytic Quarterly, Inc., 1973.*

Lewis, M.M. (1997), *Altering Fate: Why the Past Does Not Predict the Future.* Connecticut: Guilford Press.

Loeb, F.F., Jr. (1982), Generalization as a defense. *Psychoanalytic Study of the Child,* 37:388-419.

Lorenz, K. (1966), *On Aggression.* London: Methuen & Co., p. 21.

Mahler, M., Pine, F., & A. Bergman. (1975), The Psychological Birth of the Human Infant. *Symbiosis and Individuation.* New York: Basic Books.

Massie, H., & Szajnberg, N. (2005), *Lives Across Time/Growing Up: Paths to Emotional Health and Emotional Illness.* Philadelphia: Xlibris Corporation.

Mayes, L.C. (1994), Understanding adaptive processes in a developmental context: a reappraisal of Hartmann's problem of adaptation. *Psychoanalytic Study of the Child,* 49:12-35.

Mekeel, H.S. (1932), *A Modern American Community in the Light of Its Past.* Dissertation for the degree of Doctor of Philosophy, Yale University.

Moore, B.E., & Fine, B.D., eds. (1990), *Psychoanalytic Terms & Concepts.* New Haven and London: The American Psychoanalytic Association and Yale University Press.

Nachman, P.A. (1991), The maternal representation – a comparison of caregiver-and mother-reared toddlers. *Psychoanalytic Study*

of the Child, 46:69-90.
— (1998), Maternal identification: A description of the process in real time. Journal of the American Psychoanalytic Association, 46:209-228.

Novick, J., & Novick, K.K. (1996), *Fearful Symmetry: The Development and Treatment of Sadomasochism*. Northvale, N.J.: Jason Aronson.

Pestalozzi, J.H. (1894), *How Gertrude Teaches her Children*. London: Swan Sonnenschein.

Provence, S., & Lipton, R. (1962), *Infants in Institutions: A Comparison of Their Development with Family-Reared Infants During the First Year of Life*. New York: International Universities Press.

Pumpian-Mindlin, E. (1969), Vicissitudes of infantile omnipotence. *Psychoanalytic Study of the Child*, 24:213-226.

Ribble, M.A. (1943), *The Rights of Infants*. New York: Columbia University Press.

Richards, A.D., Bachant, J.L., & Lynch, A.A. (1995), Relational models in Psychoanalytic Theory, *Psychoanalytic Psychology*, 12:71-88.

Searl, N. (1929), The flight to reality. *International Journal of Psycho-Analysis*, Volume 10.

Shapiro, T. (1981), On the quest for the origins of conflict. *Psychoanalytic Quarterly*, 50:1-21.

Small, M.F. (1997), Our babies, ourselves. Natural History, 106:42-51.

Spitz, R.A. (1945), Hospitalism: an inquiry into the genesis of psychiatric conditions in early childhood. *Psychoanalytic Study of the Child*, 1:53-74.
— (1946a), Anaclitic depression. *Psychoanalytic Study of the Child*, 2:313-342.
— (1946b), Hospitalism: a follow-up report. *Psychoanalytic Study of the Child*, 2:113-117.

Spock, B. (1945), *The Common Sense Book of Baby and Child Care*. New York: Duell, Sloan, and Pearce.

Stern, D.N. (1985), *The Interpersonal World of the Infant*. New York: Basic Books.
— (1988), *The Birth of a Mother: How the Motherhood Experience Changes You Forever*. New York: Basic Books.

Talberg, G., Cuoto Rosa, J., & O'Donnell, M.L. (1988), Early affect development: Empirical research. *International Journal of Psycho-Analysis*, 69:554.

Trevarthan, C. (1979), Communication and cooperation in early infancy: A description of primary intersubjectivity. *Before Speech: The Beginning of Interpersonal Communication*, M. Bullowa (ed.), Cambridge: Cambridge University Press.

Von Hug-Hellmuth, H. (1919), *A Study of the Mental Life of the Child, Nervous and Mental Disease Monograph Series No. 29*. Washington: Nervous and Mental Disease Publishing Company.

Weber, M. (1921), *The Theory of Social and Economic Organization*. New York: Oxford University Press, 1947.

Weil, J.L. (1992), *Early Deprivation of Empathic Care*. Madison, CT: International Universities Press.

Winnicott, D.W. (1935), The manic defense. *Through Paediatrics to Psycho-Analysis*, M. Khan (ed.). London: Hogarth Press and the Institute of Psycho-Analysis, 1975, pp. 129-144.

— (1953), Transitional objects and transitional phenomena. *International Journal of Psycho-Analysis*, 34:89-97.

— (1956), Primary maternal preoccupation. *Collected Papers: Through Paediatrics to Psycho-Analysis*. New York: Basic Books, 1958, pp. 300-305.

— (1960), Ego distortion in terms of true and false self. *The Maturational Processes and the Facilitating Environment*. New York: International Universities Press, 1965, pp. 140-152.

— (1962), Ego integration in child development. *The Maturational Processes and the Facilitating Environment*. New York: International Universities Press, 1965, pp. 56-63.

— (1967), The location of cultural experience. *International Journal of Pyscho-Analysis*, 48:368-372.

Whiting, B.B. (ed.) (1963), Six Cultures: Studies of Child Rearing. New York: John Wiley & Sons.

Woodcock, L. (1941), *The Two Year Old*. New York: EP Dutton & Company.

Young-Bruehl, E. (1989), Looking for Anna Freud's mother. *Psychoanalytic Study of the Child*, 44:391-408.

www.ingramcontent.com/pod-product-compliance
Lightning Source LLC
Chambersburg PA
CBHW050705280326
41926CB00088B/2591